2010

Additional Praise for The Only Guide You'll Ever Need for the Right Financial Plan

"Larry Swedroe has given us an experienced and research-based treatment with examples of what should enter into the design and implementation of an investment strategy. The book includes a wide range of alternative investments and savings related plans that should prove to be beneficial to individuals and to their financial advisors."

—John A. Haslem, Professor Emeritus of Finance,
Robert H. Smith School of Business,
University of Maryland
Mutual funds researcher and
author of *Mutual Funds*

"*The Only Guide You'll Ever Need for the Right Financial Plan* may be the best collection of advice on key issues such as when to begin Social Security benefits and how to tax efficiently manage your money during your accumulation and withdrawal phases of life.

—Dr. William Reichenstein, CFA,
Pat and Thomas R. Powers Chair in Investment Management,
Hankamer School of Business, Baylor University

"As Larry makes abundantly clear, wise investing is wise only in the context of one's own unique personal financial situation. If you are an investor who has not considered how your investments fit into your life, you need this book."

—Edward R. Wolfe, Ph.D.,
Professor of Finance, Western Kentucky University

"Larry Swedroe has hit yet another home run with his ninth and newest book."

—W. Scott Simon, J.D., CFP®,
AIFA®, Author, *The Prudent Investor Act:
A Guide to Understanding*,
Columnist, Morningstar's Fiduciary Focus

The Only Guide You'll Ever Need for the Right Financial Plan

The Only Guide You'll Ever Need for the Right Financial Plan

MANAGING YOUR WEALTH, RISK, AND INVESTMENTS

Larry E. Swedroe

Kevin Grogan and Tiya Lim

BLOOMBERG PRESS
An Imprint of
WILEY

Published by John Wiley & Sons, Inc., Hoboken, New Jersey.

Published simultaneously in Canada.

For general information on our other products and services or for technical support, please contact our Customer Care Department within the United States at (800) 762–2974, outside the United States at (317) 572–3993 or fax (317) 572–4002.

Wiley also publishes its books in a variety of electronic formats. Some content that appears in print may not be available in electronic books. For more information about Wiley products, visit our web site at www.wiley.com.

Library of Congress Cataloging-in-Publication Data:

Swedroe, Larry E.
   The only guide you'll ever need for the right financial plan : managing your wealth, risk, and investments / Larry Swedroe, Kevin Grogan, Tiya Lim.
     p.   cm.
   Includes bibliographical references and index.
   ISBN 978-1-57660-366-6 (cloth); 978-0-470-87885-9 (ebk)
   1. Portfolio management.   2. Investment analysis.   3. Risk management.
   4. Investments.   5. Finance, Personal.   I. Grogan, Kevin.   II. Lim, Tiya.   III. Title.
   HG4529.5.S9364 2010
   332.6–dc22

                                                                                  2010014479

Printed in the United States of America.

10 9 8 7 6 5 4 3

This book is dedicated to the employees of the Buckingham Family of Financial Services and the advisers at the more than one hundred independent, fee-only registered investment adviser (RIA) firms with which we at Buckingham have strategic alliances. Each and every one of them works diligently to educate investors on how markets really work, building long-term relationships by doing the right thing.

Contents

Part III: Implementing the Plan

Part IV: The Investment Plan and Financial Security

Preface

Each of the prior eight books I have written reflects what I have learned in my almost forty years of managing financial risks for major corporations and advising individuals, institutions, and corporations on the management of financial risks.

Included among my books is the trilogy of "Only Guides." The first focuses on equities, the second on bonds, and the third on alternative investments. Each presents what one might call the "science" of investing: evidence based on peer-reviewed academic studies. The "Only Guides" explore the best investment vehicles to use, the risks and rewards of major asset classes, specific types of investments, and the benefits of a globally diversified portfolio. The books even present model portfolios, but these are meant as starting points only. Each investor has a unique ability, willingness, and need to take risk.

What investors need today is a book offering more specific investment advice, one focusing on the "art" of investing and guiding investors to adapt a winning investment strategy to their own situation. That is what this book is all about.

This "Only Guide" addresses a wide range of investment issues. For example, who should consider owning more small-cap stocks, value stocks, and emerging market stocks, and who should consider owning less of them? It also addresses the often-overlooked subjects of asset location (as opposed to allocation), withdrawal strategies in retirement, and when and how to take Social Security benefits. Most importantly, it will help you integrate other financial issues into an overall financial plan. Having a well-thought-out investment plan is a *necessary* condition for success, not a *sufficient* one. The sufficient condition is integrating the investment plan into a well-thought-out estate, tax, and risk management plan. As we demonstrate in Part IV, even the best investment plans can fail if these other issues are not adequately addressed.

The goal of this book is to help both investors and professional advisers make better, more informed decisions in order to practice the winning investment strategy. Thus, the book is designed to help you understand the fundamental concepts of asset allocation, asset location, and other investing and general financial planning concepts. After reading this book, you will have learned how to:

- design an investment policy statement (IPS) and asset allocation plan, one most appropriate to your unique situation
- locate assets in the most tax-efficient manner
- maintain the portfolio's risk profile in the most efficient manner
- provide effective tax management
- integrate risk management and estate planning issues into the plan

While written to be accessible, this is not a "dummies" book. The assumption is that you know some basics about stocks and bonds.

How to Use this Book

This book can be used in two ways: read cover to cover or searched for topics of interest, providing quick access to information to answer specific questions that may arise and as circumstances change. Thus, it can serve as a reference manual. Most topics are broad based. You will find a brief discussion of a subject and perhaps a reference to an appendix or one of my other books containing a more detailed discussion of the subject.

Because investing is more art than science, this guide is not meant to provide hard-and-fast rules. While a physicist can measure the speed of light to the fourth decimal place with minimal estimation error, even the most fervent finance professor knows that such precision is impossible in investment theory. Investors and advisers alike must accept that they will never know, *ex-ante*, the optimal allocation to international investments or how much an investor's portfolio should tilt toward value stocks or small-cap stocks. In most cases, all they can be sure of is that they are in the ballpark. This book is a tool to help you make prudent decisions, remembering prudence is determined not by the outcome, but by the process. Therefore, this book:

- raises questions leading you to the best answer given a particular situation
- helps identify issues that should be considered
- gives direction so you can best use your own judgment and apply it to each unique situation

As a final resource, the book contains an extensive glossary of terms.

LARRY SWEDROE

Acknowledgments

Books are seldom the work of one person, or in this case three people. Ours represents the collective wisdom of the investment professionals at the Buckingham Family of Financial Services.

For all their support and encouragement we would like to thank the principals of our firm: Adam Birenbaum, Ernest Clark, Susan Shackelford-Davis, Steve Funk, Bob Gellman, Ed Goldberg, Ken Katzif, Mont Levy, Steve Lourie, Vladimir Masek, Bert Schweizer III, Brenda Witt, and Stuart Zimmerman.

Too many of our co-workers contributed to list them all. But we would be remiss if we did not mention the special efforts and contributions of RC Balaban, Jim Cornfield, David Ressner, John Corn (who made major contributions to the sections on retirement plans and college savings plans) and Aaron Vickar (who made major contributions to the chapter on insurance). Jared Kizer, the coauthor of *The Only Guide to Alternative Investments You'll Ever Need*, also made important contributions. The usual caveat of any errors being our own certainly applies.

We also thank our agent, Sam Fleischman, for all his efforts.

Kevin adds: My wife, Julie, makes every day a joy. I thank her for her love and patience. I thank my parents and my brother, who have always supported me and had my best interests in mind. I owe an enormous debt to all the kind people (especially Jared Kizer and Vladimir Masek) who have taken the time to teach me what I know about investment theory.

Tiya adds: Thank you to my parents, Chak and Mira. You have supported my decisions all along the way.

I especially thank my wife, Mona, the love of my life, for her tremendous encouragement and understanding during the lost weekends and many nights I sat at the computer well into the early morning hours. She has always provided whatever support was needed. And then some. Walking through life with her has truly been a gracious experience.

LARRY SWEDROE

PART

I

INVESTMENT STRATEGY
IN AN UNCERTAIN WORLD

CHAPTER 1

The Uncertainty of Investing

When there's uncertainty, they always think there's another shoe to fall. There is no other shoe to fall.
— Kenneth Lay, former CEO of Enron

Investing deals with both risk and uncertainty. In 1921, University of Chicago professor Frank Knight wrote (he is not the publisher) the classic book *Risk, Uncertainty, and Profit*. An article from the Library of Economics and Liberty described Knight's definitions of risk and uncertainty as follows: "Risk is present when future events occur with measurable probability. Uncertainty is present when the likelihood of future events is indefinite or incalculable."

In some cases, we know the odds of an event occurring with certainty. The classic example is that we can calculate the odds of rolling any particular number with a pair of dice. Because of demographic data, we can make a good *estimate* of the odds that a 65-year-old couple will have at least one spouse live beyond age ninety. We cannot know the odds precisely because there may be future advances in medical science extending life expectancy. Conversely, new diseases may arise shortening it. Other examples of uncertainty: the odds of an oil embargo (1973); the odds of an event such as the attacks of September 11, 2001; or the odds of an accounting scandal the size of Enron. That concept is uncertainty.

It is critical to understand the important difference between these two concepts: risk and uncertainty. Consider the following example.

An insurance company might be willing to take on a certain amount of hurricane risk in Dade and Broward counties in Florida. They would price this *risk* based on perhaps one hundred years of data, the likelihood of hurricanes occurring, and the damage they did. But only a foolish insurer would place such a large bet that the company would go bankrupt if more or worse hurricanes occurred than in the past. That would be ignoring the *uncertainty* about the odds of hurricanes occurring: The future might not look like the past. [A number of insurers made this bad bet, losing big-time when Hurricane Andrew swept through Florida in 1991.]

Just as there are foolish insurance companies, there are foolish investors. The mistake many investors make is to view equities as closer to risk where the odds can be precisely calculated. This tendency appears with great regularity when economic conditions are good. Their "ability" to estimate the odds gives investors a false sense of confidence, leading them to decide on an equity allocation exceeding their ability, willingness, and need to take risk.

During crises, the perception about equity investing shifts from one of risk to one of uncertainty. We often hear commentators use expressions like, "There is a lack of clarity or visibility." Since investors prefer risky bets (where they can calculate the odds) to uncertain bets (where the odds cannot be calculated), when investors see markets as *uncertain*, the risk premium demanded rises. That causes severe bear markets.

The historical evidence is clear that dramatic falls in prices lead to panicked selling as investors eventually reach their "GMO" point. The stomach screams "Don't just sit there. Do something: Get me out!" Investors have demonstrated the unfortunate tendency to sell well *after* market declines have already occurred and to buy well *after* rallies have long begun. The result is they dramatically underperform the very mutual funds in which they invest. That is why it is so important to understand that investing is always about uncertainty and about never choosing an allocation exceeding your risk tolerance. Avoiding that mistake provides investors the greatest chance of letting their heads, not their stomachs, make investment decisions. Stomachs rarely make good decisions.

Efficient Frontier Models

To assist in the development of investment plans some investors and many advisers use what are called efficient frontier models.

Harry Markowitz first coined the term "efficient frontier" almost forty years ago. He used it to describe a set of portfolios with the highest expected return for each level of risk. Today, many efficient frontier programs are available. They begin with individual investors answering questions about their risk profiles. The program then generates a portfolio consisting of various asset classes delivering the greatest expected return given the individual's risk tolerance. Sounds like a wonderful idea. The problem is understanding the nature of an efficient frontier model and the assumptions on which it relies. As with a sophisticated racing car, a powerful tool in the wrong hands can be a very dangerous thing.

Efficient frontier models attempt to turn investing into an exact science, which it is not. For example, it is logical to believe that in the future, stocks will outperform fixed income investments. The reason is stocks are riskier than risk-free Treasury bills. Investors will demand an "equity risk premium" to compensate them for this risk. While the past may be a guide to the size of the equity risk premium, the bull market of the 1990s and bear markets of 2000–02 and 2008 demonstrate that it is no guarantee.

The equity risk premium is not constant. From 1927 through 1999, the equity risk premium was 6.8 percent. By the end of 2002, it had fallen to 5.7 percent. By the end of 2007, it was back up to 6.1 percent. And by the end of 2008, it had fallen to 5.4 percent. We shall see that even relatively small changes to the inputs are very important when it comes to efficient frontier models.

Efficient frontier models rely on inputs of expected returns, correlations, and standard deviations (measure of volatility) for each asset class that could be used in the portfolio. Let's begin with a simple portfolio that can potentially invest in just five asset classes: S & P 500 (U.S. large-cap); U.S. small-cap; one-year fixed income; Europe, Australasia, and the Far East index (EAFE) (international large-cap); and international small-cap. Table 1.1 shows our assumptions for returns, correlations, and standard deviations. Using standard deviation as the measure of risk, let us also assume we have designated a 12 percent standard deviation as the level of

Table 1.1   Capital Market Expectations

	S & P 500	U.S. Small	One-Year Fixed Income	EAFE Index	Int'l Small
S & P 500 Index	1.0				
U.S. small	0.8	1.0			
One-year fixed income	0.0	0.0	1.0		
EAFE Index	0.6	0.4	0.0	1.0	
Int'l small	0.4	0.4*	0.0	0.8	1.0
Expected return (%)	12*	14	6	12	14
Standard deviation (%)	20	30	4	20*	30

*Assumptions changed in different case scenarios, below.

portfolio risk we are willing to accept. An efficient frontier model will generate the optimal asset allocation.

The following is the recommended allocation generated by the efficient frontier model.

Case A	
S&P 500 Index	22%
U.S. Small	9%
One-year fixed income	38%
EAFE Index	22%
International Small	9%

We now make a series of minor changes to expected returns, standard deviations, and correlations to see how sensitive the efficient frontier models are to assumptions. Each change, indicated by an asterisk in Table 1.1, will be a minor one from our original base case. In Case B, we reduce the expected return of the S & P 500 from 12 percent to 11. In Case C, we increase the standard deviation of the EAFE index from 20 percent to 22 percent. In Case D, we reduce the correlation between U.S. small-caps and international small-caps from 0.4 to 0.2. In each case, the efficient frontier model generated a dramatically different asset allocation, sometimes entirely

	Case A	Case B	Case C	Case D
S & P 500 Index	22%	0%	36%	15%
U.S. small	9%	20%	4%	15%
One-year fixed income	38%	40%	40%	40%
EAFE Index	22%	36%	0%	15%
International small	9%	4%	20%	15%

eliminating an asset class from the portfolio. This implies a precision nonexistent in the field of financial economics.

We reiterate: Investing is not an exact science. It is foolish to pretend we know in advance exact levels for returns, correlations, and standard deviations. Yet that is the underlying assumption of every efficient frontier model. Experienced practitioners know that to come up with something intelligent, they must generally impose constraints on efficient frontier models. Examples of constraints might be that no asset class can either exceed 30 percent or be less than 10 percent of a portfolio. Another might be that international assets in aggregate cannot exceed 40 percent of the portfolio. The impact of imposing constraints is similar to what we would end up with using a simple common-sense approach (without the need for modeling)—a relatively balanced, globally diversified portfolio with exposure to all the major asset classes. Simply put: Don't waste your time with efficient frontier models.

CHAPTER 2

The Investment Policy Statement

*Have a plan. Follow the plan, and you'll be surprised how
successful you can be. Most people don't have a plan. That's why
it's easy to beat most folks.*

—Paul "Bear" Bryant

No rational traveler would ever take a trip to a place he has
never been without a road map and directions. Similarly, no
rational businessperson would start a business without spending lots
of time and energy thoroughly researching that business and then
developing a well-thought-out plan. Investing is no different. It is
not possible to make a rational decision about any investment without considering how the addition of that investment would impact
the risk and return of the entire portfolio, and thus the odds of
achieving the plan's objectives.

There is an old and wise saying that those who fail to plan, plan
to fail. Yet, many investors begin their investment journey without
a plan, an investment policy statement (IPS) laying out the plan's
objectives and the road map to achieving them. The IPS includes
a formal asset allocation identifying both the target allocation for
each asset class in the portfolio and the rebalancing targets in the
form of minimum and maximum tolerance ranges. A written IPS
serves as a guidepost and helps provide the discipline needed to
adhere to a strategy over time.

Just as a business plan must be reviewed regularly to adapt to changing market conditions, an IPS must be a living document. If any of the plan's underlying assumptions change, the IPS should be altered to adapt to the change. Life-altering events (a death in the family, a divorce, a large inheritance, or the loss of a job) can impact the asset allocation decision in dramatic ways. Thus, the IPS and resulting asset allocation decisions should be reviewed whenever a major life event occurs.

Even market movements can lead to a change in the assumptions behind the IPS and portfolio's asset allocations. For example, a major bull market, like the one we experienced in the 1990s, lowered the need to take risk for those investors who began the decade with a significant accumulation of capital. At the same time, the rise in prices lowered future expected returns, having the opposite effect on those with minimal amounts of capital (who were perhaps just beginning their investment careers). The lowering of expected returns to equities meant that to achieve the same expected return investors would have to allocate more capital to equities than would have been the case had returns been lower in the past. The reverse is true of bear markets. They raise the need to take risk for those with significant capital accumulation, while lowering it for those with little. A good policy is to review the IPS and its assumptions at least annually.

The Foundation of the Investment Plan

Because it outlines and prescribes a prudent and individualized investment strategy, the IPS is the foundation of the investment plan. Meir Statman, a behavioral finance professor at Santa Clara University, notes the importance of psyches in investment behavior, likening the situation to antilock brakes. "When at high speed, the car in front of us stops quickly, we instinctively hit the brake pedal hard and lock 'em up. It doesn't matter that all the studies show that when the brakes lock, we lose control." Statman suggests investors need antilock brakes for their investment portfolios as well.

Instinctively we react to investment situations in ways that might have saved our lives fighting on distant battlefields long ago. But, today they are counterproductive, like locking up our brakes. When the market drops, our instinctive fear to flight is so strong, even the most rational investors find themselves caving in, to their own demise. And market tops can often be called soon after the staunchest of bears throws in the towel and turns bullish.[1]

An IPS can act as an investor's antilock braking system. Your own IPS will provide you the discipline to stick with your plan and reduce the risk of emotions (greed and envy in bull markets or fear and panic in bear markets) from impacting the decision-making process.

Before writing an IPS, you should thoroughly review your financial and personal status. Financial situation, job stability, investment horizon, tolerance for risk, and need for emergency reserves vary from investor to investor and change over time for each individual. The IPS should not be developed in isolation. It should be integrated into an overall financial plan, one addressing investments and the entire spectrum of risk-management issues (creditor protection and the need for life, health, disability, long-term care, liability, and even longevity insurance).

The written IPS should include a list of your specific goals, such as the rate of return you are trying to achieve, the amount of additional assets you are planning on adding to your portfolio each year (assuming you are in the accumulation phase), the amount of assets you are trying to accumulate by a certain date, when you plan to begin withdrawals from the portfolio, and the dollar amount (or percentage) you plan on withdrawing each year. This will allow you to track progress toward the goal, making appropriate adjustments along the way.

The next step is to specify the asset allocation, first identifying how much will be allocated to equities and how much to fixed income. Within these two broad categories, you need to establish the appropriate percentage allocations for each of the individual asset classes, such as small cap, value, and emerging markets. Next, list the ranges within which you will allow market movements to cause the designated allocation to drift before you will rebalance the portfolio. (See Table 2.1.) The process of rebalancing is discussed in Chapter 11.

Table 2.1 Sample Rebalancing Table

Asset Class	Minimum Allocation (%)	Target Allocation (%)	Maximum Allocation (%)
U.S. large	7.5	10	12.5
U.S. large value	7.5	10	12.5
U.S. small	7.5	10	12.5
U.S. small value	7.5	10	12.5
Real estate	7.5	10	12.5
Total U.S.	45	50	55
International large value	3.75	5	6.25
International small	3.75	5	6.25
International small value	3.75	5	6.25
Emerging markets	3.75	5	6.25
Total international	15	20	25
Total equity	65	70	75
Nominal bonds	7.5	10	12.5
TIPS	15	20	25
Total fixed income	25	30	35

The Need for Plan B

Investment plans should consider both the expected returns on equities and bonds and the possibility that returns could be well below those expectations. For example, it is likely that in January 1990 few Japanese investors expected Japanese large-cap stocks to produce overall negative returns over the next nineteen years. Another example: U.S. large growth stocks produced negative returns for the ten years from 1999 through 2008—an occurrence unprecedented since 1938.

Since we know that severe bear markets are likely to occur from time to time but cannot know how long they will last, a critical part of the financial planning process is developing a contingency plan (Plan B), a plan of action implemented if a "black swan" (a major unexpected event) appears. The plan should detail what actions should be taken if financial assets fall to such a degree that investors run an unacceptably high risk of failure. For example, the portfolio may run out of assets if Plan A is not adapted to the existing reality. Or it may be that the investors have an important bequeath goal they don't want put at risk, such as a special-needs child.

Plan B should list the actions to be taken if financial assets drop below a predetermined level. Those actions might include remaining in or returning to the workforce, reducing current spending, reducing the financial goal, or selling a home and/or moving to a location with a lower cost of living. Consider the following example.

Mr. and Mrs. Brown

It is 2003, and Mr. and Mrs. Brown are each fifty years old. Mrs. Brown is a successful doctor; Mr. Brown is a college professor. They plan to retire at age sixty. Working with their adviser, they decide that their risk tolerance means holding a portfolio with a "worst case" cumulative loss of 25 percent. Thus, they decide to set their equity allocation at 60 percent. Based on historical evidence, the Browns know there is a reasonably high probability their portfolio will not experience a cumulative loss of more than 25 percent. However, they also know it is possible a greater loss could occur. A Monte Carlo simulation (see Glossary and Chapter 16) shows their plan has a 92 percent chance of success.

The mistake many investors make is to focus solely on the high odds of success and ignore the odds of failure. That is the same mistake as not buying life insurance because the odds of dying in the near future are so low. The Browns do not make that mistake. They recognize the possibility of failure exists, but they do not plan on that scenario as the "base case."

The Worst Case Should Not Be the Base Case

Using the worst case as the base case means that ability to take risk is low, so returns are going to be low. Therefore, investors making the worst case their base case will reduce risk but have significantly less to spend in retirement than if they had not done so and the worst never happened.

The Browns had worked hard, saved well, and wanted to enjoy the rewards of their efforts. But they did not ignore the risk of the possibility of "failure." They agreed with their adviser that if a bear market occurred, resulting in a new Monte Carlo simulation producing odds of success of less than 85 percent, they would consider taking some or all of the following steps, depending on the size of their losses:

- sell their second home
- reduce their daily spending requirements by 10 percent
- reduce their travel budget by 50 percent
- continue working until at least age sixty-five
- move to a region with a lower cost of living

While the Browns hoped they would never have to execute any of these steps, they did recognize the risk that it could be necessary, and they were prepared to do so.

Only list options you are actually prepared to take. Listing ones you really won't exercise will cause you take too much risk in the first place. Write down your options. It will help you determine which ones are truly real.

Returning to our example, for the next five years the Browns lived well and enjoyed their lifestyle. When the 2008 financial crisis hit, they were well prepared to take the steps needed to prevent their plan from failing.

PART

II

ASSET ALLOCATION

CHAPTER 3

Asset Allocation

In their well-known textbook, *Investments*, Zvi Bodie, Alex Kane, and Alan Marcus define asset allocation as "the distribution of risky investments across broad asset classes." Taking a broader view, asset allocation can be defined as the process of investing assets in a manner reflecting one's unique ability, willingness, and need to take risk. Consider these as three different tests.

The Ability, Willingness, and Need to Take Risk

The Ability to Take Risk

An investor's ability to take risk is determined by four factors: (1) investment horizon, (2) stability of earned income, (3) need for liquidity, and (4) options that can be exercised should there be a need for "Plan B."

Let's begin with the issue of the investment horizon. The longer the horizon, the greater is the ability to wait out the virtually inevitable bear markets. In addition, the longer the investment horizon, the more likely equities will provide higher returns than fixed-income investments.

Table 3.1 provides a *guideline* for this part of the ability to take risk.

Investment horizon is not the only consideration: The individual's labor capital must be considered. This asset is often overlooked because it does not appear on any balance sheet.

An investor's ability to take risk is impacted by the stability of their earned income. The greater the stability of earned income, the

17

Table 3.1   Ability to Take Risk

Investment Horizon	Maximum Equity Allocation (%)
0–3 years	0
4 years	10
5 years	20
6 years	30
7 years	40
8 years	50
9 years	60
10 years	70
11–14 years	80
15–19 years	90
20 years or longer	100

greater the ability to take the risks of equity ownership. For example, a tenured professor has a greater ability to take risk than either a worker in a highly cyclical industry where layoffs are common or an entrepreneur owning a business with cyclical earnings. The tenured professor's earned income has bond-like characteristics. All other things being equal, she has more ability to hold equity investments. The entrepreneur's earned income has equity-like characteristics. He should hold more fixed income investments.

For some investors, particularly those with high net worth or approaching retirement, labor capital may be a very small part of their overall wealth. For such investors, labor capital considerations should have less impact on the asset allocation decision.

A third factor impacting the ability to take risk is the need for liquidity. The need for liquidity is determined by the amount of near-term cash requirements as well as the potential for unanticipated calls on capital. The liquidity test begins by determining the amount of cash reserve one requires to meet unanticipated needs for cash, such as medical bills, car or home repair, or job loss. Financial planners generally recommend a cash reserve of about six months of ordinary expenses.

The fourth factor impacting the ability to take risk is the presence (or absence) of options one can exercise should a severe bear market create the risk the investment plan will fail. As we discussed in the section on the need for a Plan B, options include delaying retirement, taking a part-time job, downsizing the current home, selling a second home, lowering consumption, or moving to a region with a lower cost of living. The more options, the more risk one can take.

The Willingness to Take Risk

The willingness to take risk is determined by the "stomach acid" test. Ask yourself this question: Do you have the fortitude and discipline to stick with your predetermined investment strategy when the going gets rough? To a large degree, successful investment management depends on the investor's abilities to withstand periods of stress and overcome the severe emotional hurdles present during bear markets like the ones experienced in 1973–74, 2000–02, and 2008–09.

Table 3.2 provides a guideline for investors to test their willingness to take risk.

Table 3.2   Willingness to Take Risk

Maximum Tolerable Loss (%)	Maximum Equity Exposure (%)
5	20
10	30
15	40
20	50
25	60
30	70
35	80
40	90
50	100

The Need to Take Risk

The need to take risk is determined by the rate of return required to achieve the investor's financial objectives. The greater the rate of return needed to achieve one's financial objective, the more equity (and/or small and value) risk one needs to take. A critical part of the process is differentiating between real needs and desires. These are very personal decisions with no right answers. The fewer things falling into the needs column, the lower the need to take risk. Conversely, the more things fall into the needs column, the more risk one will have to take to meet the need. Therefore, in considering the financial objective, carefully consider what economists call the marginal utility of wealth: how much any potential incremental wealth is worth relative to the risk that must be accepted in order to achieve a greater *expected* return. While more money is always better than less, at some point most people achieve a lifestyle with which they are very comfortable. At that point, taking on incremental risk to achieve a higher net worth no longer makes sense: The potential damage of an unexpected negative outcome far exceeds any benefit gained from incremental wealth. Put another way: "The inconvenience of going from rich to poor is greater than most people can tolerate. Staying rich requires an entirely different approach from getting rich. It might be said that one *gets* rich by working hard and taking big risks, and that one *stays* rich by limiting risk and not spending too much."[1]

Each investor needs to decide at what level of wealth their unique utility of wealth curve starts flattening out and begins bending sharply to the right. Beyond this point, there is little reason to take incremental risk to achieve a higher *expected* return. Many wealthy investors have experienced devastating losses that could easily have been avoided if they had had the wisdom to know what author Joseph Heller knew. Kurt Vonnegut told this story about his fellow author:

"Heller and I were at a party given by a billionaire on Shelter Island. I said, 'Joe, how does it make you feel to know that our host only yesterday may have made more money than your novel *Catch-22* has earned in its entire history?' Joe said, 'I've got something he can never have.' And I said, 'What on earth could that be, Joe?' And Joe said, 'The knowledge that I've got *enough*.'"

The lesson about knowing when enough is enough can be learned from the following incident. In March 2003, Larry was in Rochester, Minnesota, for a seminar based on his book, *Rational Investing in Irrational Times: How to Avoid the Costly Mistakes Even Smart People Make.* During his visit, he met with a seventy-one-year-old couple with financial assets of $3 million. Three years earlier, their portfolio had been worth $13 million. The only way they could have experienced that kind of loss was if they had held a portfolio that was almost all equities and heavily concentrated in U.S. large-cap growth stocks, especially technology stocks. They confirmed this. They told Larry that they had been working with a financial adviser during this period—demonstrating that while good advice does not have to be expensive, bad advice almost always costs you dearly.

Larry asked the couple if, instead of their portfolio falling almost 80 percent, doubling it to $26 million would have led to any meaningful change in the quality of their lives. The response was a definitive no. Larry commented that the experience of watching $13 million shrink to $3 million must have been very painful and that they probably had spent many sleepless nights. They confirmed his observation. He then asked why they had taken the risks they did, knowing that the potential benefit was not going to change their lives very much but that a negative outcome like the one they had experienced would be so painful. The wife turned to the husband and punched him, exclaiming, "I told you so!" Some risks are not worth taking. Prudent investors do not take more risk than they have the ability, willingness, or need to take. Think about it this way: If you've already won the game, why still play?

When Conflicts Arise

When analyses of your ability, willingness, and need to take risk all lead to the same conclusion, the asset allocation decision is easy. However, there are often conflicts. For example, one can have a high ability and willingness to take risk but little need. In that case, the answer is simple: Because the marginal utility of wealth is likely low, the need to take risk should dominate the decision. Sometimes the choices are more difficult. Consider the following situation.

Philip is an extremely nervous investor. His willingness to take risk would probably produce an equity allocation approaching zero. He knows, however, that a very low equity allocation is apt to produce very little, if any, growth in the real value of his portfolio. This directly conflicts with his personal objective to retire within ten to fifteen years. To attain this objective, Philip knows he must take more risk, so chooses an equity allocation of at least 80 percent. The lower the equity allocation, the longer he would have to continue in the workforce. His willingness to take risk proved to be in direct conflict with his personal goals. Larry told Philip there was no correct answer to this conundrum. He would have to choose which of his objectives would have greater priority—the need to sleep well or the desire for early retirement. Ultimately, Philip decided his early retirement objective should take priority. He realized this decision was apt to produce those sleepless nights and that his ability and willingness to stay the course might be sorely tested.

Choosing the higher equity allocation (taking more risk) was the right choice for Philip, but it might not be the right choice for you. In general, we recommend choosing the lowest equity allocation derived from the three tests and then altering your goals. For example, if you find you have a higher need to take risk than your ability or willingness suggests, your plan should use the lower equity allocation recommended by the ability and willingness to take risks. Otherwise, if the risks show up—in the form of bear markets or negative events such as divorce or job loss—the plan will fail, and you may not be able to successfully adapt to the change in circumstances. The alternative is to lower your goal and save more now and/or plan on working longer. As discussed earlier, the more options one has, the more risk one can take. Having said that, before taking a higher level of risk, make sure you are truly willing to exercise those options. While it may be possible to move to a lower cost of living area, if your spouse doesn't want to leave the grandchildren, it won't happen.

The tables provided in this chapter are useful tools, good starting points for deliberations on the asset allocation decision, but many other factors influence that decision. The following sections provide application examples to help you make the appropriate recommendation. Use of a Monte Carlo simulator, explained in Chapter 16, is also recommended for determining your asset allocation.

Risk Factors

The fundamental concept of risk and return in equity investing is embodied in what is known as the Fama-French three-factor model, named after professors Eugene F. Fama and Kenneth R. French. The model states that the returns one can expect from a diversified equity portfolio are virtually unrelated to either the ability to pick stocks or timing the market. Instead, it is the degree of exposure to three *risk factors* that explains the majority of returns.

The first risk factor is the portfolio's exposure to the overall stock market. Since equities are riskier than fixed-income investments, they must provide higher *expected* returns. Note that when discussing risk premiums financial economists use annual (arithmetic mean), not annualized (compound) returns. From 1927 through 2008, the average annual equity risk premium—the return above riskless one-month Treasury bills—has been 7.5 percent.

The second risk factor is the size of a company as determined by market capitalization. Intuitively, we know that small companies are riskier than large companies. They have provided an annual risk premium of 3.0 percent over large companies.

The third risk factor considers "value." High book-to-market (BtM) value stocks are intuitively riskier than low BtM growth stocks. They have provided an annual risk premium of 5.0 percent over growth stocks.

Studies have verified the existence of these risk premiums in international markets and emerging markets, as well as domestic markets and have found that the premiums are similar in size.

Every equity portfolio has some degree of exposure to each of the three risk factors. The equity to fixed-income allocation, small-cap stock to large-cap stock allocation, and value stock to growth stock allocation decisions are the all-important determinants of the risk and return of a portfolio.

Fama and French's factor model indirectly tells us that stocks, bonds, and other investments fall into separate asset classes (real estate versus commodities, for example) because they possess unique systematic risk and return characteristics. Conversely, the three-factor model tells us the decision of how much to allocate to different sectors (financial sector versus health care sector) is probably not as important because health-care stocks are not a separate asset class from stocks in general. Sectors do not have truly unique systematic risk and return characteristics.

Similarly, developed foreign markets are different from emerging markets. And allocations to individual countries (Germany versus Japan) are probably not as important. German or Japanese stocks are not a separate asset class from developed foreign-market stocks in general.

The following sections are designed to help you with these all-important allocations decisions. In each case, we will examine the reasons why investors should consider increasing or decreasing their exposure to an asset class. Examples are provided to illustrate the points made.

CHAPTER

4

Equities

Equities versus Fixed Income

This is the most important asset allocation decision and the primary
determinant of the expected return and risk of an investor's portfolio. We will now examine reasons why an investor should consider
having a higher or lower equity allocation.

Reasons to Increase Equity Exposure

- **Longer time horizon.** Younger investors have more human
  capital (more future labor income) to offset investment risk. In
  addition, investors with longer horizons have the ability to "wait
  out" a bear market without being forced to sell in order to meet
  cash-flow needs. This is especially true for investors who are still
  working. The longer your time horizon, the less likely equities
  will underperform fixed income investments.
- **High level of job stability.** This is particularly true for individuals with income from jobs having little or no correlation
  to the economic risks of equity investing and the economy
  in general. A doctor or a tenured professor has income with
  bond-like characteristics. The income of an entrepreneur,
  whose business is affected by the performance of the stock
  market or does poorly when the economy is doing poorly, has
  equity-like characteristics.
- **High tolerance for risk.** These individuals may have a full
  understanding and faith that in the long run, they will likely

be compensated with higher returns for the increased risk. Or they may simply not watch their accounts closely. Most importantly, they are willing to accept the consequences if returns are well below those of safe fixed-income investments.

- **Need for higher returns to reach financial goals.** In these cases, the willingness and ability to take risk should be carefully evaluated against the need to ensure that the investor fully understands the implications. An alternative to taking extra risk would be to either cut current consumption (providing more investment capital) or to revise goals to ones that are less financially demanding.
- **Retirees with multiple streams of stable income (pension and Social Security income) that are relatively high compared to needs.** We can view these streams of income as quasi-fixed-income exposure. High-net-worth investors may also have other streams of income affecting the allocation process.
- **High marginal utility of wealth.** Those whose next dollar earned provides a high marginal utility will have a high willingness and perhaps a high need to take risk.
- **Ability to adjust the "supply" of human capital.** Consider the following: You develop a financial plan allowing you to retire at age sixty-five. But the market's return falls below the expected return, or you don't save as much as you expected. You need to work longer. The questions: Will you have the ability to continue in the labor force? What level of income will you be able to generate? Will the market allow you to sell your skills and at what price? Younger workers typically have more ability to adjust their supply of human capital. Those with a variety of skill sets also have a greater ability to adjust their supply to economic conditions. Those with more ability to adjust their supply of human capital can take more equity risk.
- **The presence of options one can exercise should a severe bear market create the risk the investment plan will fail.** The more options one has, the more risk one can take. It is critical to only include options one is actually prepared to exercise.

Reasons to Reduce Equity Exposure

The reasons to reduce equity exposure are the opposite of those above, with one additional issue to consider: Human capital should have less impact on appropriate allocations for retirees or high-net-worth investors, who typically have no earned income or minimal earned income relative to their net worth.

Here are some examples of how to apply the above guidelines.

Application: For a young business owner, the effect of a longer time horizon could be offset by the high correlation of the business owner's job and income prospects with the performance of the equity markets. Therefore, this young business owner might have a more conservative asset allocation than a young doctor with similar risk tolerance.

Application: Consider two retirees who are similar in every respect (age and risk tolerance) except for their sources of noninvestment income. The first retiree has both Social Security income and pension income from a very stable source. The second has only Social Security income. In this case, the first retiree could afford to be more aggressive with his investable assets.

Application: We have two doctors similar in every respect, including working at the same hospital, having the same risk tolerance, and performing the same type of job. The only relevant difference is age. The guidelines would say the older doctor should have a more conservative allocation. However, if they have the same current wealth and financial goals, the older doctor has less time to achieve those goals and thus has a higher need to take risk. The doctor will have to decide if the need to take risk or ability and willingness to take risk should dominate the decision. There is no right one answer, just one right for each individual.

Application: Two individuals are similar in all respects except one has a low tolerance for risk. The person with the lower risk tolerance becomes nervous and is unable to sleep well whenever the financial markets are in turmoil. This individual is more prone to panicked selling and should have a lower equity allocation.

Application: Two individuals are similar in all respects with the exception that one wishes to leave a large estate to a charitable organization or heirs. The other has a significantly lower bequeath motivation. The individual with the motivation to leave a large estate has a higher marginal utility of wealth and should have a higher equity allocation.

Application: Other things being equal, an investor with a primary goal of not running out of money in retirement should consider a lower equity allocation than one whose primary goal is to leave a large estate.

Application: A high-net-worth individual with a relatively low spending requirement should consider a lower equity allocation, even if they have a long investment horizon, stable job, and high level of tolerance for risk.

U.S. Equity versus International Equity

Investing in international stocks, while delivering expected returns similar to domestic stocks, provides the benefit of diversifying the economic and political risks of domestic investing. There have been long periods when U.S. stocks performed relatively poorly compared to international stocks. The reverse has also been true. Over the long term, returns have been similar. Thus, the gains from international diversification come from the relatively low correlation among international securities. This is especially important for those employed in the United States, as it is likely their labor capital is highly correlated with domestic risks.

The logic of diversifying economic and political risks is why investors should consider allocating *at least* 30 percent and as much as 50 percent of their equity holdings to international equities. To obtain the greatest diversification, benefit exposure to international equities should be unhedged: Hedging the currency risk increases the correlation of returns to U.S. equities.

Reasons to Increase International Equity Exposure

Reduced Risk. The historical evidence suggests that raising the international allocation to at least 40 percent reduces portfolio risk (volatility).[2] But for many people, increasing the international equity exposure above 50 percent of the total equity portfolio does not make sense because of tracking-error concerns and from a risk-return perspective. Both are addressed in the discussion below.

Investor Has Non−U.S. Dollar Expenses. An investor may live part of the year overseas or frequently travel overseas. The investor should consider tailoring the portfolio to gain specific exposure to the currency in which the expenses are incurred. This could also be accomplished by making fixed-income investments in the local currency.

Reasons to Decrease International Equity Exposure

Tracking Error. Tracking error is defined as underperformance versus a benchmark. Some investors may not be able to stomach the tracking error associated with a portfolio with 40 percent of its equity invested overseas.

Table 4.1 illustrates tracking error risk by comparing the performance from 1991 through 2008 of a portfolio with a 100 percent allocation to U.S. stocks (S&P 500 Index) to the performance of a portfolio with a 60 percent allocation to U.S. stocks and 40 percent allocation to international stocks (MSCI EAFE Index).

While investors are pleased when there is positive tracking error (2002−07), many cannot tolerate underperforming their peers by significant margins when the tracking error turns negative (1995−98). Unless investors can tolerate negative *tracking error* and rebalance when appropriate, an international allocation will not be of much value.

Table 4.1   1991−2008

	S&P 500 (%)	MSCI EAFE (%)	60% S&P 500/ 40% MSCI EAFE (%)	Portfolio Return Minus Return of S&P 500 (%)
1991	30.5	12.5	23.2	−7.2
1992	7.6	−11.8	−0.2	−7.8
1993	10.1	32.9	19.2	9.1
1994	1.3	8.1	4.0	2.7
1995	37.6	11.6	27.2	−10.4
1996	23.0	6.4	16.3	−6.7
1997	33.4	2.1	20.8	−12.6
1998	28.6	20.3	25.3	−3.3
1999	21.0	27.3	23.5	2.5
2000	−9.1	−14.0	−11.1	−1.9
2001	−11.9	−21.2	−15.6	−3.7
2002	−22.1	−15.7	−19.5	2.6
2003	28.7	39.2	32.9	4.2
2004	10.9	20.7	14.8	3.9
2005	4.9	14.0	8.6	3.7
2006	15.8	26.9	20.2	4.4
2007	5.5	11.6	8.0	2.4
2008	−37.0	−43.1	−39.4	−2.4

Sources: Standard & Poors (S&P 500 Index), MSCI Barra (MSCI EAFE Index).

Costs Matter

While international assets provide an important diversification benefit, international investing is more expensive because of higher trading costs and higher fund expenses. Allocating more than 50 percent to international equity may not be optimal from a risk-return perspective. An exception might be an investor whose labor capital risk is substantial. Tilting heavily toward international equity can diversify that risk.

Recommended Reading

To learn more about the benefits of international investing read Chapter 4 of *The Only Guide to Alternative Investments You'll Ever Need.*

Emerging Markets

Emerging markets comprise those nations whose economies are considered developing or emerging from underdevelopment, including almost all of Africa, Eastern Europe, Latin America, Russia, the Middle East, and much of Asia, excluding Japan, Hong Kong, and Singapore. Many investors shy away from emerging markets, viewing them as either highly risky investments or pure speculations. The riskiness of emerging markets should not preclude investors from allocating some portion of their portfolio to them. Modern portfolio theory (MPT) tells us that sometimes we can add risky assets and actually reduce the risk of the overall portfolio. The reason is the diversification benefit.

Another reason to consider investing in emerging markets is that because it is a risky asset class, an efficient market will appropriately price that risk. The result is higher expected returns. Historical evidence shows that emerging market equities have high returns with high volatility. They also have low correlations to both domestic and international equities. And the evidence shows that including a small amount of emerging markets equity in a portfolio increases that portfolio's return while leaving volatility roughly the same.

Reasons to Increase Emerging Markets Equity Exposure

Increased expected return. The primary reason to increase one's allocation to emerging markets is to increase the expected return of the portfolio. Investors who need to increase their expected return to meet their financial goals can use an allocation to emerging markets to help meet this objective.

Reasons to Decrease Emerging Markets Equity Exposure

Tracking error. Emerging markets equity has a relatively low correlation with both the overall U.S. markets and international developed markets. Therefore, emerging markets' returns may be below their average when the U.S and/or other developed markets are producing above-average returns. Some investors may not be able to tolerate this tracking error. Also, the correlation of emerging markets equity could be high enough in some periods that inclusion of a large allocation (greater than 10 percent of the equity allocation) to emerging markets could actually increase the volatility of the overall portfolio to an unacceptable level.

The correlation of emerging markets to other equity asset classes typically rises during periods of financial turmoil. Thus, when the low correlation is most needed, the correlation is likely to increase. Investors who are either highly sensitive to tracking error risk or highly risk averse should consider limiting their exposure to emerging markets.

Recommended Reading

To learn more about the benefits of investing in emerging markets, read Chapter 4 of *The Only Guide to Alternative Investments You'll Ever Need.*

Value versus Growth

The value versus growth decision is another important allocation choice investors need to make. When thinking about the guidelines below, remember that the market portfolio is completely neutral with respect to value and growth exposure. It is neither value- nor growth-tilted.

Most investors with value-tilted portfolios choose to do so for one of three reasons. They believe:

1. Value stocks are riskier than growth stocks. Therefore, value stocks should provide a risk premium in the same way that equities should provide a risk premium over the return of

safer fixed-income investments. This is the traditional finance point of view.

2. Value stocks are *not* riskier than growth stocks. They believe investors systematically overprice growth stocks and under-price value stocks. The value premium is a free lunch, not a risk premium. They argue that value stocks provide superior risk-adjusted returns than growth stocks. This is the behavioral finance point of view. Behavioralists use the Internet and technology bubble of the late 1990s to bolster their argument.

3. Both traditionalists and behavioralists are partially right: Value stocks are riskier than growth, but the risk premium has been too large to be explained by the excess risk. While it may not be a free lunch, it just might be a free stop at the dessert tray.

We will assume the traditional financial view of the value premium to be a risk story, but it is helpful to be aware of all viewpoints.

Reasons to Increase Value Exposure

Increased expected return with increased risk. From a traditional finance point of view, investors should tilt toward value if they need to increase the expected return of their portfolios to meet their goals—but only if they are willing and able to accept the incremental risk of value stocks.

Diversification of sources of risk. Consider an investor needing a certain rate of return to achieve his goals. That rate of return can be achieved with a certain exposure to beta (total stock market) risk. The appropriate allocation to the total market (which has no value exposure) might be 60 percent. Another way to achieve the same goal is to lower the exposure to beta (50 percent) but add sufficient value exposure so that the two portfolios have the same expected return. Historically, the value-tilted portfolio with a lower exposure to beta has exhibited less volatility. The reasons are that the value premium has been less volatile than the equity premium and has low correlation to the equity risk premium. (Appendix A provides further explanation.)

Application: A high-net-worth investor with a low marginal utility of risk may still want to achieve a certain return. The downside risk of the portfolio can be reduced by lowering the exposure to beta while increasing the exposure to the value premium. The trade-off is a lower probability of producing returns above the expected.

Application: An individual whose labor capital has a low correlation to the value premium should consider increasing their exposure to value stocks. Typical examples are tenured professors, doctors, and retirees. Another good candidate for increasing the exposure to value stocks is a high-net-worth investor whose labor capital is a low percentage of his overall net worth.

Reasons to Decrease Value Exposure (or Maintain a "Market" Exposure)

Reduced risk. Those taking the traditional finance point of view believe in tilting towards growth stocks to reduce portfolio risk. Investors who are exposed to value risk factors in ways other than investments should use this strategy. This includes owners of distressed businesses, employees and top-level managers of value companies, as well as retirees who receive (or in the future will receive) pension benefits from a value company. For this type of investor, a neutral exposure to value or even a growth tilt (compared to the market) is more appropriate.

Tracking error. Portfolios tilted toward value will not move in lockstep with the overall market. Investors with value-tilted portfolios must be able to stomach the tracking error occurring during the inevitable periods of value underperformance. Depending on the investor, a more neutral exposure to value might make sense.

Application: An owner or employee of a value company (a company with a high BtM ratio) should probably not tilt as heavily toward value stocks as a tenured professor. Other individuals who should consider not tilting to value stocks (or limiting their tilt) are construction workers, automobile workers, or any employee or owner of a highly cyclical business. For these investors, a neutral exposure to value or even a growth tilt (compared to the market) might be more appropriate.

Small-Cap versus Large-Cap

Considerations on how much to invest in small-cap stocks versus large-cap stocks are basically the same as for the value versus growth decision. Small-cap stock risk tends to appear during periods of economic distress, which is when value stocks also tend to perform poorly. Large-cap stocks tend to perform better during these periods because large companies have more diverse sources of capital, are less likely to be cut off from those sources, and are less prone to bankruptcy.

Reasons to Increase Small-Cap Exposure

Increased expected return with increased risk. Investors should tilt toward small-cap stocks if they need to increase the expected return from their portfolios to meet their goals—but only if they are willing and able to accept the incremental risk of small-cap stocks.

Stable human capital. Investors not particularly exposed to economic-cycle risk might consider tilting their portfolios toward small-cap stocks. Doctors, tenured professors, and retirees with defined benefits generally fit this description. Advertising company executives, construction workers, and most commissioned salespeople are more exposed to this type of economic-cycle risk.

Diversification of sources of risk. As was discussed in the value section, tilting more to small-cap stocks maintains the expected return of the portfolio while lowering the exposure to beta. This reduces the potential dispersion of returns. The diversification benefit arises from the low correlation of the size risk factor to both the market risk and value risk factors. (Appendix A provides further explanation.)

Reasons to Decrease Small-Cap Exposure

Less stable human capital. Tilting toward large-cap stocks might be a valid strategy for investors vulnerable to periods of economic distress. Investors whose business, employment, or income might be negatively affected by a poor economy might want to tilt toward larger, safer stocks.

Lower risk. Tilting toward large-cap stocks reduces the volatility of a portfolio. Risk-averse investors and those with a low marginal utility of wealth may prefer to focus on reducing volatility as opposed to maximizing returns.

Application: You are a small business owner whose company tends to do poorly when the overall economy does poorly. With inherent exposure to small-cap risk, you might want to tilt toward large-cap stocks.

Real Estate

Academic studies demonstrate that both domestic and international equity real estate investment trusts (REITs) offer an attractive risk/

return trade-off and provide meaningful diversification benefits to portfolios. The reasons equity real estate should be considered a core asset are:

- REITs reduce the overall risk of the portfolio by adding an asset class that responds to events differently from other asset classes: Its correlation to other asset classes is low
- REITs have expected returns well above the risk-free rate
- As real assets, REITs provide a reasonably good long-term hedge against unexpected inflation
- Adding an allocation to REITs allows investors to create a portfolio more reflective of the overall investment universe.

There are two ways to gain real estate exposure: (1) through directly owned real estate; (2) through REITs, using a product like Vanguard's REIT mutual fund. REITs are the stocks of companies having real estate operations. Both forms of real estate exposure should be expected to lower the volatility of an equity-only portfolio.

Domestic REITs have low correlation to both domestic and international equities. International REITs have even lower correlation to domestic equities and low correlation to other international equities. Thus, both domestic and international REITS are excellent diversifiers of equity risks.

Reasons to Increase Real Estate Exposure

Lower portfolio volatility. REITs and directly owned real estate have low correlation with most other asset classes. This is true of both domestic and international REITs.

Increase the income return of the portfolio. Since REITs are required to pay out most of their annual earnings, they could be beneficial for a charitable remainder trust (CRT).

Reasons to Decrease Real Estate Exposure

- **Individuals who already have fairly diversified real estate exposure.** If they already have it, through their business or other investments, they might not need additional real estate exposure.
- **Increased tracking error.** An allocation to real estate increases the tracking error of the portfolio relative to broad-market indices.

- **Tax inefficiencies associated with REITs.** REITs are prime candidates for tax-deferred accounts. See Chapter 10.
- **No "best" place to hold international REITs.** Because their dividends are nonqualified, they should not be placed in taxable accounts unless one is in the lowest tax brackets. Conversely, because of the loss of the foreign tax credit (FTC), the cost of holding them in tax-advantaged accounts is increased. The cost of losing the FTC is about 9 percent of the dividend yield.

Your Home

A primary residence is clearly real estate, but it is very undiversified real estate. First, it is undiversified by type. There are many types: office, warehouse, industrial, multi-family residential, hotel, and unimproved land. Owning a home provides exposure to just the residential component of the larger asset class of real estate. Even by excluding multi-family residences, it is only exposure to the single-family component. Second, a home is undiversified geographically. Home prices might be rising in one part of the country and falling in another. Third, home prices may be more related to an exposure to an industry than to real estate in general. For example, in the 1980s, home prices in Texas and in oil-producing regions in general collapsed when oil prices collapsed. One's home provides some exposure to real estate but not diversified exposure.

A home is a very different financial asset. You cannot perform the normal portfolio maintenance tasks such as rebalancing and tax management. While clearly an asset with value that should appear on the balance sheet and be considered a possible source to fund future cash-flow needs (through a reverse mortgage or sale), it should be excluded from consideration when thinking about asset allocation.

Recommended Reading

To learn more about the benefits of real estate investing, read Chapter 1 of *The Only Guide to Alternative Investments You'll Ever Need.*

Collateralized Commodity Futures (CCF)

Commodities fall within the broad category of hard assets and are an interesting class from a portfolio perspective. While a highly volatile asset class, from 1970 through 2008 they have exhibited negative correlation with both equities and bonds.

The expected return of fully collateralized commodity futures is probably only marginally higher than that of safe investments like high-quality fixed income. However, the combination of commodities' high volatility and negative correlation to equities and nominal return bonds historically results in less risky, more efficient portfolios. Those including commodities have produced higher risk-adjusted returns. Adding small amounts of commodities to a portfolio has reduced volatility without negatively impacting compound returns in a significant way. Commodities are worthy of consideration for inclusion in a globally diversified portfolio.

Investors should consider an allocation to CCF of between 5 and 10 percent of their equity allocation.

Reasons to Increase Commodity Futures Exposure

The primary reason to add commodity futures to a portfolio is to reduce the overall volatility of that portfolio without the negative impact on returns produced by adding fixed-income assets. This may seem counterintuitive because commodity futures themselves are very volatile, but historically commodity futures have had negative correlation with most every other major asset class. Negatively correlated assets act like portfolio insurance. Including them reduces potential dispersion of returns, reducing the opportunity for greater than expected portfolio returns while lowering the risk of less than expected ones.

Candidates for Higher Commodity Allocations

- **Risk-averse investors.** The more risk averse, the greater the allocation to commodities—but no more than 10 percent of the portfolio.
- **Those in the withdrawal phase of their investment careers.** Volatility negatively impacts the odds of a portfolio running out of money for any given withdrawal rate. Being negatively correlated with other portfolio assets, adding commodities reduces portfolio volatility, reducing the odds of a portfolio running out of money while simultaneously reducing the odds of leaving a large estate. Retirees and endowments are prime candidates for considering higher commodities allocations.

- **Investors exposed to the risks of unexpected inflation.** This includes both individuals on fixed income (fixed annuities or pensions) and those owning longer-term bonds.
- **Investors needing greater return from their fixed income investments than short-term bonds can provide.** In these circumstances, it is better to take duration risk rather than credit risk. CCF can hedge the risks of longer-term bonds.
- **Investors concerned about event risks that could negatively impact equities and nominal return bonds.**

Adding commodities to a portfolio increases the odds of success in Monte Carlo simulations. Even a 3 to 5 percent allocation will generally improve the odds of success by about 2 percent. The offset is that the allocation reduces the odds of achieving a very large estate. The allocation to commodities should be taken from the equity allocation. If taken from the fixed-income allocation, portfolio volatility will increase, defeating the main purpose of reducing such risk.

Application: Investors who have recently retired may want to reduce the volatility of their portfolios. Adding commodities has historically produced that result.

Reasons to Decrease Commodity Futures Exposure

Risk-tolerant investors or investors needing a high return to reach their financial goals may not be willing to give up expected return in exchange for lowering portfolio volatility. Furthermore, the addition of CCF increases tracking error risk. Perhaps most importantly, commodities should be considered only by those able to view the results of the whole portfolio, ignoring returns of the component parts. While to some degree this is true of all assets with low correlation, it is especially true in the case of CCF, which are highly volatile and have relatively low expected returns compared to the equities they displace in a portfolio. Due to the tax inefficiency of CCF, they should not be included in taxable accounts but in tax-deferred accounts. See Chapter 10 for more details on asset location.

Application: A young investor in the early stages of accumulation may not want to sacrifice expected return for lower volatility. This type of investor might choose to exclude commodities and accept higher volatility.

Recommended Reading

To learn more about commodities as an asset class, read Chapter 3 of *The Only Guide to Alternative Investments You'll Ever Need.*

Socially Responsible Investing (SRI)

SRI has been referred to as "double-bottom-line" investing. You are seeking both profitable investments and those meeting your personal ethical standards. You sleep with a clear conscience. Some investors don't want their money supporting companies that sell tobacco products, alcoholic beverages, or weapons, or companies that rely on animal testing as part of their research and development efforts. Other investors may be concerned about social, environmental, governance, labor, or religious issues. SRI encompasses many personal beliefs, not one set of values.

SRI funds cannot be endorsed if the sole criteria are investment-related issues. They add incremental costs (higher expense ratios) and are less effectively diversified. They are inefficient investments. However, for those investors willing to pay a price for investing according to their values, passively managed funds should be used to implement an SRI strategy. A subset of SRI is typically referred to as "sustainability" or "green" investing (see Glossary).

Recommended Reading

To learn more about SRI, read Chapter 10 of *The Only Guide to Alternative Investments You'll Ever Need.*

CHAPTER

5

Fixed Income

In this chapter, we address the roles of fixed-income investments in a portfolio and offer recommendations on credit quality and maturity. We also discuss inflation-protected securities and investing in municipal bonds.

Credit Quality

The main roles of fixed-income assets in a portfolio are reducing *portfolio* risk to the level appropriate for the investor's unique circumstances and providing a reliable source of cash flow. Therefore, fixed-income assets should generally be limited to AAA/AA investment grades. When we refer to ratings, we are referring to what can be called a "natural" rating: those not enhanced by either an insurer adding their guaranty or by collateral acting as a credit enhancement (as is the case with most asset-backed securities). Historically, credit risk has not been well rewarded.

Bank certificates of deposit (CDs) can also offer competitive rates relative to other high-quality, short-term–fixed-income assets. To eliminate credit risk, CDs under a single account name at a single bank should not exceed the Federal Deposit Insurance Corp. (FDIC) limits. For additional information, please see the FDIC's "Guide to Deposit Insurance Coverage."

Hybrid securities such as high-yield bonds, convertible bonds, preferred stocks, and emerging-market bonds should be avoided. They all have equity-like risks managed more efficiently with direct investments in equities.

41

Short-Term versus Long-Term Maturities

Short-term bonds have the benefit of less volatility and lower correlation to equities. Long-term bonds should provide higher returns to compensate for the additional risk. The question is whether investors are compensated for taking on additional risk by extending the maturity of fixed-income assets. We evaluated the use of short-term bonds (one-year Treasuries), intermediate-term bonds (five-year Treasuries) and long-term bonds (twenty-year Treasuries), finding that the most efficient maturity depends on the investor's overall asset allocation.

For portfolios with the commonly used allocation of 60 percent equities (split 60 percent domestic and 40 percent international) and 40 percent bonds, the highest Sharpe ratio (risk-adjusted return) has been achieved with five-year Treasuries. Extending maturities to twenty years produced higher returns, but a lower Sharpe ratio (a result of their higher volatility and higher correlation to equities). While risk-seeking investors might prefer the portfolio with long-term bonds, most investors are risk averse.

Short-term bonds have less volatility and lower correlation to equities than long-term bonds. Shifting from long-term to short-term does not allow an investor to increase the Sharpe ratio by increasing the equity allocation to achieve higher returns with the same volatility. The shorter maturity does not allow the investor to take more risk on the equity side of the allocation.

Another thing risk-averse investors should consider is that the longer the maturity, the longer "left tail" (larger losses) in the distributions of annual returns.

The Results at Different Equity Allocations

The appropriate maturity varies depending on the equity allocation. At equity allocations below 80 percent, five-year Treasuries produced the most efficient portfolios, though long-term bonds produced the portfolios with the highest returns. At high equity allocations (80 percent or higher), the portfolio with long-term Treasuries produced the highest return and highest Sharpe ratio.

At high equity allocations, the higher returns from longer-term bonds dominate the effect of the higher standard deviation: The volatility of equities is the dominant factor in the portfolio's volatility. At high fixed-income allocations the reverse is true: The high standard deviation of longer-term bonds dominates the higher returns.

Reasons to Reduce Maturity Risk

- Investors focusing on volatility, and not risk-adjusted returns, should minimize maturity risk.
- Investors with a high fixed-income (low equity) allocation should hold shorter-term bonds to minimize overall portfolio risk.
- Investors highly exposed to inflation risk should hold short-term nominal return bonds or Treasury inflation-protected securities (TIPS).

Reasons to Increase Maturity Risk

- Investors with a high equity allocation should consider holding longer-term bonds (assuming the yield curve is positively sloped), as the volatility of the portfolio will be dominated by the equity holdings. The higher the equity allocation, the more duration risk one should consider taking.
- Investors seeking higher returns who are willing to accept the risks of longer-term bonds should consider extending maturities, so long as the yield curve is positively sloped (so that they are compensated for taking incremental risks).
- Investors who have an allocation to collateralized commodities futures should consider extending maturities. Commodities have negative correlation to longer-term bonds, acting as a hedge against the inflation risk of longer-term bonds.
- Investors more exposed to the risks of deflation than inflation, such as commissioned sales people, should consider extending maturities of nominal return bonds.
- Investors with known fixed-rate, long-term liabilities should consider matching those liabilities with long-term fixed instruments.
- Investors concerned about reinvestment risk should consider extending maturities.

Application: Younger investors with fixed income allocations may be able to tilt toward longer-term fixed income if their job income can be expected to increase with inflation. Those living on fixed-income sources should generally avoid longer-term bonds.

Recommended Reading

For more detailed information on this topic, read "The Maturity of Fixed Income Assets and Portfolio Risk" in the Winter 2009 edition of *The Journal of Investing*.

Municipal Bonds

Taxable fixed-income investors, except those in the lowest tax brackets, should prefer to hold municipal bonds. However, there are times when even investors in the lowest tax brackets should consider owning municipal bonds.

Maturity Risk

Because the yield curve for municipal bonds is generally steeper than for taxable bonds, it may be appropriate to extend the maturity of municipal bonds further than would be the case for taxables.

Credit Risk

As with taxable bonds, holdings should be limited to AAA/AA. It is important that the rating investors rely on is that of the issuer, not an insurer.

Inflation-Protected Securities

Inflation-protected securities are also known as *real* return bonds because they provide a guaranteed real (inflation adjusted) return. Real return bonds offered by the U.S. Treasury convey the following benefits:

- Insulating investors from risks of unexpected inflation.
- Having real returns less volatile than real return of nominal return bonds of similar maturity.
- Lower correlations to equities than nominal return bonds, making them more effective diversifiers of equity risk. In fact, the correlation of TIPS to equities has been negative.
- No credit risk.

The U.S. government issues two types of real return bonds: Treasury inflation-protected securities (TIPS) and I-bonds. TIPS are sold at auction and receive a fixed, stated real rate of return.

The principal is adjusted for inflation before the fixed-interest payment is calculated. Like TIPS, I-bonds provide a fixed real rate of return and an inflation-protection component. While the instruments are similar, there are some differences. The fixed rate on an I-bond is announced by the Treasury in May and November and applies to all I-bonds issued during the subsequent six months. Like zero-coupon bonds, their total return (fixed rate plus inflation adjustment) accrues in value. I-bonds increase in value on the first of each month and compound semiannually. They pay interest for up to thirty years. They can be bought and redeemed at most financial institutions. The redemption value can never go below par. All income is deferred for tax purposes until the investor withdraws funds from the account holding the bond. Due to limitations on the purchases of I-bonds, we will focus our analysis on TIPS.

Academic papers analyzing TIPS benefits all reach a similar conclusion: TIPS should dominate the fixed-income portfolios of most investors, at least for assets in tax-advantaged accounts.

Reasons to Increase Exposure to TIPS

- The future liabilities of most investors are real liabilities: the costs of goods and services rising with inflation. For such investors, nominal bonds become the risky asset. The risk shows up if future inflation is greater than expected. For such investors, TIPS should dominate their tax-advantaged, fixed-income allocations.
- Since TIPS have negative correlation to equities, the greater the equity allocation, the more investors should prefer TIPS.

Reasons to Decrease Exposure to TIPS

- The future liabilities of some investors are nominal in nature. Consider a defined-benefit pension plan, the future obligations of which are fixed in nominal dollars. For such a plan, the riskless instrument is a Treasury bond matching the maturity of its known fixed obligations. Owning inflation-indexed bonds creates the risk of having insufficient assets to meet obligations. The risk develops if future inflation is less than expected.
- Investors whose labor capital is likely to rise with inflation might consider a higher allocation to nominal bonds. While

investors are working, it is likely that their wages will at least keep pace with inflation. There is less need for TIPS, which provide protection against unexpected inflation.

- Investors more exposed to the risks of deflation than inflation should prefer long-term nominal return bonds.
- If taxes are of particular concern, investors with few dollars in tax-deferred accounts may prefer short-term municipal bonds. If the municipal bond yield curve is steep, they should also consider extending maturities.

Short-Term Fixed Income versus TIPS

Short-term, high-quality fixed income investments and TIPS are similar in one important respect: Both protect an investor against increases in inflation. TIPS provide direct protection. Because they mature in the near future, short-term, high-quality fixed income investments provide indirect protection: Higher inflation leads to higher short-term rates. An important difference between the two is that TIPS lock in a real rate of return while the real rate of return on short-term fixed income will fluctuate. So, TIPS— not short-term fixed income—should be considered the risk-free investment for long-term investors. Academic research concludes that for tax-advantaged accounts, TIPS should dominate the fixed-income portion of the portfolio, unless the risk premium for unexpected inflation is high (greater than fifty basis points).

There is no liquid-futures market for inflation, so we cannot directly observe the market's estimate of inflation or precisely know the size of the risk premium for unexpected inflation. We can suggest at least a way to *estimate* its size. First, suppose TIPS yield 2.0 percent and nominal Treasuries yield 4.5 percent. The 2.5 percent difference reflects both expected inflation and an uncertainty premium in the yield of nominal bonds. Next, look at the consensus forecast of inflation by economists provided by the Federal Reserve Bank of Philadelphia (www.phil.frb.org/research-and-data). If it is 2 percent, the difference of 0.5 percent (2.5 percent minus 2.0 percent) is an approximation of the uncertainty premium.

Because TIPS come in various maturities, investors need to decide on a strategy. If they invest in a mutual fund or exchange-traded fund (ETF), they need to know the average maturity of the fund's holdings. If the fund is managed as an index of TIPS, the maturity will average

Table 5.1   Decision Table for Allocation and Maturity of TIPS

Real Yield on TIPS (%3)	Allocation of Total Fixed Income to TIPS (%)	Maturity of TIPS in years
>3	75–100	Twenty+
>2.5 < 3	50–75	Fifteen
>2 < 2.5	25–50	Ten
>1.5 < 2	0–25	Five
>1.5	0	Two years or less

around ten years. Investors purchasing individual TIPS must decide on a specific maturity. One strategy is to build a laddered portfolio of individual TIPS, diversifying maturity risk. Another is to shift maturities based on current yields and their relationships to the long-term real return of nominal bonds. Table 5.1 is a tool for determining the portion of fixed income to be represented by TIPS and their maturities when purchasing individual TIPS. You can create your own, but some table is needed to maintain investment discipline.

Recommended Reading

To learn more about TIPS, read Chapter 2 of *The Only Guide to Alternative Investments You'll Ever Need*. To learn more about fixed-income investing in general, read *The Only Guide to a Winning Bond Strategy You'll Ever Need*.

CHAPTER

Alternative Investments

The search for better-performing assets usually leads investors to explore the broad category of alternative investments, a term generally used to describe investments outside the familiar categories of equities, Treasury bonds, other high-quality investment-grade debt and bank instruments such as certificates of deposit (CDs). This chapter focuses on the most commonly used alternative investments and provides recommendations on which should be considered.

Convertible Bonds: Not Recommended

A convertible bond gives the holder the option—the right, but not the obligation—to exchange a corporate bond for a predetermined number of shares of common stock in the issuing company, creating the perception that an investor can enjoy the best of both worlds. If the stock does well, the holder can convert to equity. If it does poorly, the investor retains the "safety" of the bond and coupon payment. The market recognizes that this option has value: The interest rate on the convertible bond is less than it would be on a similar nonconvertible debt issue.

Here's why convertible bonds are not recommended:

- As discussed in the fixed income section, bonds rated below AA are not recommended. Most convertibles fall below that level.
- The bonds of companies below the highest investment grades of AAA and AA actually contain equity-like risks. Equity

risks can be obtained more efficiently via common stock ownership.

- If the stock of a convertible issuer is doing poorly, the safety of the interest and principal payments may also be in jeopardy. There is an increasing risk, both of downgrades negatively impacting valuation and of default. You might have the *worst* of both worlds: a below-market coupon and a deteriorating credit rating.
- Call risk limits upside potential.
- Investors with a choice of asset location will be holding either the bond risk or the equity risk in the wrong location. Location issue is the subject of Chapter 10.
- They are complex instruments, the complexity designed in favor of the issuer.
- The need to diversify both the credit and stock risks involved with convertible bonds means a mutual fund is the only appropriate investment vehicle for these securities. This requirement results in an additional layer of expenses in the form of management fees that buyers of Treasury securities can avoid, since there is no credit risk, and, therefore, no need for diversification.

If the reason for buying convertibles is to seek higher returns than nonconvertible bonds can provide, the more effective strategy is either increasing the equity allocation or increasing exposure to equity classes with higher expected returns, such as small-cap stocks, value stocks, and emerging market stocks. If the reason for buying convertibles is to reduce the overall risk of the equity portfolio, it is wiser to purchase nonconvertible investment-grade bonds.

Recommended Reading

To learn more about convertible bonds, read Chapter 13 of *The Only Guide to Alternative Investments You'll Ever Need*.

Covered Calls: Not Recommended

A covered-call strategy involves investors writing (or selling) a call option on stocks already in their portfolios. In doing so, the option seller gives up all potential for appreciation above the option strike price. In exchange, the seller receives an upfront premium. If the call expires without being exercised, the portfolio return is based on the call premium and the value of the stock the call writer still owns. If the call is exercised, the call writer receives the call premium and surrenders the stock at the strike price.

While a covered-call strategy has some attraction, the negatives outweigh the benefits. For example, while a covered-call strategy provides the benefit of reducing the risk of "fat tails," or kurtosis (see Glossary), it eliminates the potential for the good fat tail (the highly positive return), while having no impact on the risk of the bad fat tail (the extremely negative return). This approach only reduces the size of the bad fat tail by the amount of the premiums collected. Risk-averse investors would much prefer the reverse.

Other negatives include tax inefficiency and trading costs. A more efficient strategy is reducing the equities allocation and increasing the allocation to high-quality fixed-income assets, while at the same time increasing exposure to value and small-cap stocks—riskier stocks with higher expected returns. Volatility and downside risk are reduced, while returns are achieved in a more tax-efficient manner. In addition, most of the potential upside is maintained.

Recommended Reading

To learn more about covered calls, see Chapter 9 in *The Only Guide to Alternative Investments You'll Ever Need*.

Fixed-Income Currency Exposure: Generally Not Recommended

Currency risk has no expected return. There is no evidence of persistent ability to generate profits from currency speculation. Investors should not use these instruments to make speculative bets on the direction of particular currencies against the dollar.

Investors seeking the diversification benefits of foreign-currency exposure can obtain those same benefits by investing in international equities that are unhedged for exchange-rate risk. On the fixed-income side, investors generally seek stability of the value of those assets, allowing them to take equity risk. Adding currency risk to fixed-income investments increases their volatility. Unhedged foreign-currency exposure for fixed-income investments is not generally recommended. On the other hand, some investors—such as those living part-time in a foreign country or planning to retire to a foreign country—may be sensitive to the prospect of a falling dollar. Such investors may benefit from hedging their dollar exposure by allocating part of their fixed-income portfolio toward achieving this hedge.

EE Bonds: Recommended

EE bonds are Treasury instruments and, like all Treasury instruments, are recommended for consideration in a portfolio. While they have a maturity of thirty years, the interest earned is based on the yield on the five-year Treasury note. Rates are announced each May and November, with the yield set at 90 percent of the average yields on five-year Treasury securities for the preceding six months. That becomes the annual rate applying to bonds for the next six-month earning period.

One reason to consider EE bonds is the special tax benefit available for education savings. For those qualifying, all or part of the interest earned on EE bonds can be excluded from taxable income when the bonds are redeemed to pay for post-secondary tuition and fees.

Recommended Reading

To learn more about EE bonds, see pages 96–99 of *The Only Guide to a Winning Bond Strategy You'll Ever Need.*

Emerging Market Bonds: Not Recommended

Investing in international bonds exposes you to a mixture of risks that are different for each country. A country's unique set of risks (political, economic, and cultural) make up what is collectively called its sovereign risk. This is the risk of a country defaulting on its debts denominated in foreign currencies. U.S. Treasury bonds entail no risk of default for U.S. investors. Default risk, however, is a real threat in emerging markets. Countries have defaulted on foreign-denominated debt because of their inability to generate sufficient foreign currency to repay their obligations.

Emerging market debt is a risky asset class, characterized by extreme volatility. Emerging market debt is similar in nature to high-yield bonds and possesses some of the same characteristics risk-averse investors find unattractive about the high-yield asset class. Among the negative features:

- They are illiquid assets.
- There is the potential for large losses: They exhibit negative skewness and high kurtosis (see Glossary).
- While having low correlation to other asset classes, the correlation of risk to equities tends to turn high at the wrong time: when equities are in distress and investors look to their bond portfolios to provide stability.
- Returns are earned in a tax-inefficient manner.
- Implementation costs are high. Mutual funds are needed, and they are expensive.

Those investors seeking exposure to the diversification benefits of investing in emerging markets should seek that exposure via equity investments. Due to the risky nature of the asset class, an investment in emerging market bonds should be considered an allocation to the asset class of equities.

Recommended Reading

To learn more about emerging market bonds, see Chapter 14 in *The Only Guide to Alternative Investments You'll Ever Need.*

Equity-Indexed Annuities (EIAs): Not Recommended

Like convertible bonds, EIAs supposedly provide "the best of both worlds": potential rewards of equity investing without the downside risks (because of the guaranteed minimum return). The typical EIA has the following characteristics:

- A link to a *portion* of the positive changes in an index (typically the S&P 500). This percentage of the index's gain is called the participation rate. Participation rates vary, but they are typically between 50 and 100 percent.
- Principal protection.
- A minimum rate-of-return guarantee, regardless of index performance.
- Tax-deferred growth potential.

- Income options to meet investors' specific needs.
- A death benefit guaranteeing beneficiaries 100 percent of the annuity's indexed value.

However, these products have so many negatives no one should consider investing in them. The high fees, commissions, tax inefficiency, penalties for early withdrawal, and their design make them unsuitable investments. All complexity favors the issuer by reducing potential payouts.

The only real benefit of the EIA is the guarantee, which applies only if the EIA is held for at least ten years. During severe bear markets, when the guarantees are the most valuable, the ability of the insurers to honor the guarantees may be in question.

Recommended Reading

To learn more about equity-indexed annuities, see Chapter 18 in *The Only Guide to Alternative Investments You'll Ever Need.*

Gold: Not Recommended

The main reason investors consider including exposure to gold is as a hedge against inflation. However, while gold has been a "store of value" over the *very long term* (the real return being close to zero), gold *may not* provide that benefit even then. For example, in January 1980, gold traded at $850 an ounce. Twenty-nine years later—a period during which inflation averaged 3.55 percent—gold was trading at roughly $900 an ounce, a return of less than 0.2 percent a year. During this particular period, an investment in gold would have lost about 3.4 percent per annum in real terms, even before investment costs. Gold is too volatile to serve as an inflation hedge.

On the positive side, gold does have very low correlation to stocks and bonds and has provided a hedge against some "event risks." This is also true of a diversified commodities fund. All things considered, there is no compelling reason to include gold in a well-diversified portfolio.

Hedge Funds: Not Recommended

Hedge funds differ from mutual funds in several ways.

- Typically, there is a lack of transparency of strategy and holdings.
- Management has limited regulatory oversight.

- They are generally available only to high-net-worth individuals.
- Unlike the typical broadly diversified mutual fund, they generally have highly concentrated large positions in just a few securities.
- They have broad latitude to make large bets, long or short, on almost any type of asset, be it a commodity, real estate, currency, country debt, or stocks.
- Management generally has a significant stake in the fund.
- Management has strong financial incentives, translating into high costs for investors. Fees typically range from 1 to 2 percent per annum, plus 20 percent of profits.

Hedge fund managers seek to outperform market indices such as the S & P 500 by exploiting what they perceive as market mispricings. The problems:

- Because of the lack of transparency of strategy and holdings, investors lose control of the risks they take.
- There is no evidence of persistent ability of managers in a particular style classification to earn returns in excess of their style benchmark.
- On a risk-adjusted basis, hedge funds have had a hard time keeping up with the returns of Treasury bills.
- They exhibit negative skewness and excess kurtosis, traits investors prefer to avoid.
- They are highly illiquid.
- They tend to be tax inefficient.
- The incentive structure creates "agency risk" (see Glossary).

It is worth noting that hedge funds also use the term "absolute return funds." The implication is they will provide solid returns in both bull and bear markets. But from 2003 through 2008, the HRFX Index of hedge funds gained just 0.7 percent per annum, underperforming every single major equity asset class, domestic and international, underperforming all high-quality fixed-income investments as well.

Recommended Reading

To learn more about hedge funds, see Chapter 15 in *The Only Guide to Alternative Investments You'll Ever Need.*

High-Yield (Junk) Bonds: Not Recommended

High-yield bonds have lower credit ratings—below BBB from Standard and Poor's and below Baa from Moody's—and higher yields than more creditworthy securities. Those higher yields are compensation for an investor's willingness to take incremental risks. Investors should not make the mistake of confusing yield with return. Part of that higher yield includes an expectation of default. In addition, most higher-yield bonds have call provisions: Investors require incremental yield for accepting the risk that the bond will be called prior to maturity.

As has been discussed, fixed-income instruments play three primary roles in a portfolio: (1) serving as a liquid reserve in the event of emergencies; (2) generating a stable cash flow; and (3) providing portfolio stability, allowing investors to take equity risk. High-yield bonds are too risky and too highly correlated with equity risk to serve these purposes. There are other negative characteristics:

- In general, investors have not been rewarded for taking credit risk. For the thirty-year period from 1979 to 2008, the Vanguard High-Yield Fund provided investors with a return of 6.31 percent per year. For the same period, the Barclays Capital U.S. Intermediate Credit Bond Index, an index of *investment grade* bonds with maturities of one to ten years, returned 8.47 percent per year. Only with short-term maturities have investors been rewarded for taking credit risk.
- They exhibit negative skewness and excess kurtosis, two traits creating the potential for large losses.
- They are hybrid securities, their returns explained by a combination of equity risk and bond risk. The lower the credit rating and the longer the maturity of the debt, the more equity-like the high-yield security becomes. This creates a location problem (discussed in Chapter 10) for those taxable investors in high-yield bonds who have a choice of location, as they will be holding either the equity risk or the bond risk in the wrong location.
- While the correlation of returns of high-yield bonds to equity assets is low, the correlations tend to turn high when equities are distressed. The perfect example of that was in 2008.

Global equities had one of the worst years ever and the Vanguard High-Yield Fund experienced a loss of over 21 percent.
Funds invested in lower-grade bonds experienced even
greater losses.
* Because of the need to diversify the unique, idiosyncratic risk
of the issuers, a mutual fund should be used. This increases
expenses even if using Vanguard's low-cost fund.

Those investors seeking higher returns can do so more efficiently by adding a bit more equity risk to their portfolio or by
adding more size and/or value risk. Historically, that has produced
more efficient results. Investors who do allocate to this asset class
should adjust their asset allocation to reflect the hybrid nature of
these instruments. The following percentage allocation to equities should be considered based on the average credit rating of
a fund: 20 percent for BB, 30 percent for B and 50 percent for
CCC.[1] Investors failing to make that adjustment may find they have
exceeded their risk tolerance.

Recommended Reading

To learn more about high-yield bonds, see Chapter 7 in *The Only
Guide to Alternative Investments You'll Ever Need.*

Leveraged Buyouts (LBOs): Not Recommended

LBOs involve a private equity firm purchasing a public company,
after which they generally take it private. When making their
acquisitions, the private equity fund will typically employ minimal amounts of its own equity and use large levels of debt, hence
the term "leveraged buyout." When the company is resold, the high
leverage creates an opportunity for incremental returns on the limited amount of equity.

Historically, after all fees and expenses, LBOs have not outperformed the S&P 500 Index despite taking far more risk. In addition
to poor performance, LBO investments are highly illiquid. Thus,
investors have not been compensated with incremental returns
for taking the liquidity risks. Investors seeking higher returns have
superior alternatives, including adding size and value exposure to
their equity allocations, or even adding their own leverage. This latter course, however, is not recommended either.

To learn more about leveraged buyouts, see Chapter 16 in *The Only Guide to Alternative Investments You'll Ever Need.*

Leveraged Funds: Not Recommended

Leveraged funds are intended to increase, multiply, or magnify the return of an investment through the use of borrowings (or derivatives such as futures contracts and options) that the fund uses to increase its total investment. Over the long term, these funds have provided poor risk-adjusted returns.

Recommended Reading

To learn more about leveraged funds, see Chapter 20 in *The Only Guide to Alternative Investments You'll Ever Need.*

Master Limited Partnerships (MLPs): Not Recommended

MLPs are typically engaged in transportation, storage, and retail energy distribution. As an asset class, MLPs exhibit low correlation to both bonds and equities. Historically, they have provided returns appropriate for the risks entailed. However, there is no good way to obtain low-cost, diversified access to the asset class. The available alternatives all carry total expenses that are too high.

Mortgage-Backed Securities (MBS): Not Recommended

MBSs are sometimes called "mortgage pass-through certificates." The reason is that the security passes through the mortgage principal and interest payments to investors at a specific coupon. It also passes through any prepayments (unscheduled payments of principal). An investor in an MBS owns an undivided interest in a pool of mortgages serving as the security's underlying asset. As an MBS holder, the investor receives a pro rata share of the cash flows from the pool of mortgages.

The MBS has a higher stated yield compared to other forms of fixed-income investments of comparable credit quality. The higher yields are compensation for greater risk, in the form of credit risk, interest rate risk, and, since maturity is uncertain, maturity risk. The one exception for credit risk is MBSs issued by Ginnie Mae (GNMA), which carry the full faith and credit of the U.S. Treasury.

MBSs have *asymmetric* price risk: The investor has sold a continuous call to the borrower because the borrower has the right to prepay at any time. The life of the MBS will be shorter than expected if interest rates fall, refinancings exceeding expectations. If rates rise, the expected life of the MBS will lengthen, borrowers extending expected stays in their current homes and leaving the lender earning below market rates. The price the owner of the MBS receives for accepting both risks is the incremental yield over a Treasury bond with the same maturity as the *expected* average maturity of the MBS on its issuance. That incremental yield is a risk premium. The only way the investor collects that risk premium is if rates stay in a relatively narrow band. Otherwise, he gets the worst of all worlds. When rates rise, he is holding an investment whose duration is lengthening at just the wrong time. When rates fall, he is holding an investment whose duration is shortening at just the wrong time. Looking at an MBS in isolation, this risk is even greater than it seems: The risks of MBS can show up at exactly the wrong time in relation to what is happening with your equity holdings.

If an investor finds the risks acceptable, it is recommended that investments be limited to GNMAs.

Recommended Reading

To learn more about mortgage-backed securities, read Chapter 9 of *The Only Guide to a Winning Bond Strategy You'll Ever Need.*

Precious Metals Equities (PME): Not Recommended

PMEs are stock investments in companies mining gold, silver, and platinum. PMEs are equities, exposed to the risks of equity investing. Though we would expect PMEs to provide returns similar to equities, in the long run they have provided returns below those of the overall equity market.

PMEs have had low correlations to both U.S. equities and international equities, been negatively correlated to intermediate-term bonds, and positively correlated with inflation.[2] Like collateralized commodity futures, they have occasionally provided stability to portfolios during periods of financial distress. However, there are some additional negatives to consider.

The first is that PMEs are highly volatile, often experiencing severe drops. Investors considering including PMEs in their portfolios must be prepared for such periods. The second is that as a "safe harbor" investment, PMEs tends to experience long periods of very low returns during periods of economic and political stability. Investors must be highly disciplined and patient. On the other hand, PMEs do experience short periods of very high returns, typically in times of crisis. It is in these periods of crises that investors have the most need to generate high returns.

Another negative is that there are currently no investment vehicles allowing you to access the asset class of PME that are low cost and low turnover.

All things considered, there is no compelling reason to include PMEs in a well-diversified portfolio.

Recommended Reading

To learn more about precious metals equities, see Chapter 11 in *The Only Guide to Alternative Investments You'll Ever Need.*

Preferred Stocks: Not Recommended

Preferred stocks are technically equity investments. However, their dividends are paid before any dividends are paid to owners of the common stock. While preferred shareholders receive preference over common-equity holders, in the case of a Chapter 11 bankruptcy all debt holders have to be paid before any payment can be made to the preferred shareholders.

Unlike common stock, which may benefit from the potential growth in the value of a company, the investment return on preferred stocks is usually a function of the stock price and the *fixed* dividend yield, although some variable preferreds are available. The difference between conventional bonds and preferred stocks is that conventional bonds have a fixed maturity date while preferred stocks may not. There are other negatives:

- They have longer maturities than appropriate for most investors. Preferred stocks are either perpetual or generally long term, with maturities typically between fifteen and thirty

years. In addition, many preferred-stock issues with a stated maturity of thirty years include an issuer option to extend for an additional nineteen years.
- There is call risk, which tends to show up at the wrong time, as when equities are in distress.
- They entail credit risk, which generally goes unrewarded.
- Dividends can be cut or suspended.
- They are hybrid securities, with equity-like characteristics— the lower the credit rating, the more equity-like the investment. Hybrid securities create location problems for some taxable investors (see Chapter 10).
- The credit risk should be diversified. A mutual fund, not individual holdings, is the only appropriate way for individuals to invest in preferreds. But using a fund adds to expenses, reducing returns.
- There are no low-cost, passively managed funds available.
- They can be highly complex securities, with the complexity designed in favor of the issuer.

In summary, the risks incurred when investing in preferred stocks make them inappropriate investments for individual investors.

Recommended Reading

To learn more about preferred stocks, see Chapter 12 in *The Only Guide to Alternative Investments You'll Ever Need.*

Private Equity (Venture Capital): Not Recommended

The term "private equity" is often used to describe various types of privately placed (as opposed to publicly traded) investments. Within the broad category of private equity, there are three major subcategories: venture capital, leveraged buyouts (LBOs), and mezzanine financing.

With its allusion to privately available opportunities, even the name of this alternative asset class is tantalizing. Individual investors may yearn to be players in an arena dominated by institutional investors such as the Yale Endowment. With all their expenses and incentive fees, private equity investments have generally failed to deliver on their promise. The high returns earned by private equity investors have not been commensurate with the incremental risks.

In fact, private equity returns have been similar to or below the returns of similarly risky publicly available equities (risky small-value stocks). Only the riskiest private equity investments—early stage venture capital—have outperformed publicly available securities.

With private equity, investors forgo the benefits of liquidity, transparency, broad diversification, and access to daily pricing enjoyed by mutual fund investors. Finally, the distributions of returns looks like a lottery ticket: Relatively high average return reflects the small possibility of truly outstanding return and the much larger probability of more modest or negative return.

Private equity investing is an unattractive proposition for the average investor.

Recommended Reading

To learn more about private equity (venture capital), see Chapter 8 in *The Only Guide to Alternative Investments You'll Ever Need.*

Stable-Value Funds: Generally Not Recommended

Stable-value investments are fixed-income investment vehicles offered through defined-contribution savings and profit-sharing plans, as well as 529 college savings plans. The assets in stable-value funds are generally bonds and insurance contracts. They are purchased directly from banks and insurance companies, sellers that guarantee to maintain the value of the principal and all accumulated interest. They deliver the desired safety and stability by *attempting* to preserve principal and accumulated earnings. The evidence demonstrates that stable-value funds have produced higher returns than short-term fixed-income instruments and have done so with similar risk.

While the returns data is attractive, problems of lack of transparency make these complex investments inappropriate for investors unable to perform the required due diligence, such as analyzing (1) the risk profile (credit rating, maturity, individual bond structure, and liquidity) of the individual securities held in the portfolio; and (2) the credit rating of the insurance providers. Few if any investors have the skills and resources to do what is required to make an informed judgment. However, they may be the best fixed-income choice for investors in retirement plans: a superior alternative to high-cost, actively managed funds.

For those able to perform the necessary due diligence, the following are offered as criteria for an acceptable investment:

- The vehicle should carry contracts with multiple, high-quality insurers: insurers carrying a rating of at least AA or the equivalent from one of the major rating agencies.
- More than 90 percent of the portfolio should be covered with insurance contracts.
- At least 90 percent of the vehicle's assets should be in investment-grade bonds, rated at least AA.
- The average maturity and duration of assets should be short term (not longer than three years).
- If the portfolio uses derivatives, there should be a thorough understanding of their usage and whether any leverage is involved.
- The fund's management team should have a record of producing returns that are competitive with its stable-value peers or an appropriate bond market index.

Recommended Reading

To learn more about stable-value funds and tips on due diligence, refer to Chapter 6 in *The Only Guide to Alternative Investments You'll Ever Need.*

Structured Investment Products: Not Recommended

Structured products are packages of synthetic investment instruments specifically designed to appeal to needs that investors *perceive* are not being met by available securities. As a result, they are often packaged as asset-allocation tools to reduce portfolio risk.

Structured products usually consist of an actual note plus a derivative or spinoff product. This second product derives its economic value by linking to the price of another asset, typically a bond, commodity, currency, or equity. A derivative often takes the form of an option (a put or a call). The note pays interest at a set rate and schedule, and the derivative pays off at maturity.

Structured products are often promoted to investors as "debt securities." Depending on the specific structured product, full protection of the invested principal may be offered. In other cases, there may be limited protection or no protection at all.

These investments come with fancy names like Accumulators, Reverse Convertibles, STRATS, Super Track Notes, and a variety of forms of Principal Protection Notes. Having reviewed dozens of these products over the years, we have yet to see one with features making it worthy of investment consideration. There have always been more efficient alternatives to achieve the same objective. These products are meant to be sold, not bought.

Before purchasing any security, an investor should consider the transaction from the perspective of the *issuer*. The issuers of structured notes are generally large, sophisticated financial institutions who are not in the business of playing Santa Claus to investors. They don't issue securities with higher borrowing costs than they would otherwise have to pay. Investors need to ask themselves: Why do these firms issue these securities? The answer is obvious: The issuers have structured the securities to generate large profits for themselves, not for investors.

If a security looks like it has a high yield or high return, then there is a high degree of risk involved. Even if you cannot see the risk, you can be sure it is there.

It is highly recommended that investors avoid the whole category of structured notes.

Recommended Reading

To learn more about structured investment products, see Chapter 19 in *The Only Guide to Alternative Investments You'll Ever Need*.

Variable Annuities: Not Recommended

A variable annuity (VA) is similar to a mutual fund account wrapped inside an insurance contract. VAs are purchased by making either a single outlay or series of payments. VAs differ from fixed payout annuities because the latter guarantee that a *specific* sum of money will be paid each period, generally monthly, regardless of fluctuations in the value of the annuity issuer's underlying investments. The value of a VA—thus, the amount that can ultimately be withdrawn—will fluctuate over time. In addition, unlike with a fixed annuity, the typical VA offers many different investment options. Typically, these are mutual funds called subaccounts, which can be managed by firms other than the issuer.

There are three investment-related motivations for considering the purchase of a variable annuity. First, as an insurance contract, its structure allows investment earnings to grow on a tax-deferred basis. Second, there is a life-insurance component, varying from product to product. Third, the investment contract can be converted into a lifetime annuity at a future date.

A fourth, non-investment-related reason for considering the purchase of a VA is creditor protection. Many states—New York, Florida, and Texas among them—protect assets in VAs from creditors. As these laws are complex, consult an attorney before purchasing (or getting talked into) a VA for this specific purpose. Doctors worried about malpractice suits, for example, might want to consider VAs, but they should be sure to purchase the right kind of annuity.

While VAs have some positive attributes, the negatives far exceed the benefits.

Although annuities allow for tax-deferred growth of earnings, that benefit usually comes at a high price. The first problem: Annuities convert what would otherwise be long-term capital gains into ordinary income. Second, the investment choices inside the typical VA are actively managed, so they tend to have high expenses. The historical evidence indicates high fees for below-benchmark performance. In addition, each fund usually levies an account charge of $10 to $25 per year. Total charges can exceed 3 percent, compared to the 0.1–0.2 percent total cost for some passive equity investments such as index funds. If you are going to purchase a VA, make sure you investigate the costs associated with the VA and its investment choices. Other negatives:

- Holding equities inside of a VA causes the loss of other tax benefits. These include the loss of the potential for a step-up in basis for the estate of the investor; the inability to harvest losses; the inability to donate appreciated shares to charity; and, if you hold international securities in your portfolio, the loss of the foreign tax credit (see Glossary).
- There is a penalty for early withdrawal. Should the buyer need unanticipated liquidity prior to age 59½, distributions will be subject to an additional 10 percent tax penalty, unless the distribution takes the form of a life annuity.

- While a typical simple return-of-premium death benefit is worth just a few basis points, the median mortality and expense-risk charge for a return-of-premium VA is in excess of 1 percent.[3] Only 5 percent of contracts have insurance charges of less than even 0.75 percent, and 12 percent of contracts charge more than 1.40 percent.[4] The insurance benefit is far exceeded by its cost. As further evidence of these excessive costs, consider that in any given year only 0.4 percent of VA contracts are surrendered on account of death or disability.[5] And only a small fraction of those reflect losses triggering a death benefit.
- Most VAs are sold with "back-end loads," otherwise known as surrender charges, which generally cover the cost of the commissions paid to the sales force. Although the charges typically decline over time, they can reach up to 10 percent and can last for as long as 15 years. There is nothing good about surrender charges.
- Buyers of annuities accept the credit risk and overall financial strength of the insurance company issuing the contract—their guarantee is only as good as their credit. Each state does provide a limited guaranty should the insurer default. Each state sets its own limit, the contracts can be rewritten, and only the principal is actually protected. It is important to note that the credit risk applies only to the insurance component of the VA, not the underlying investments. This is an important consideration given the long time frame involved, as credit risk increases with time.

Recommended Reading

To learn more about structured investment products, see Chapter 17 in *The Only Guide to Alternative Investments You'll Ever Need.*

CHAPTER

7

Liabilities and Asset Allocation

Most investors make the mistake of focusing solely on the left-hand side of the balance sheet, their assets. They tend to ignore the right-hand side. This chapter briefly addresses the issues related to the liability side of the balance sheet. We begin with the home mortgage, as it is the largest debt obligation for most individuals.

Mortgages

Most people use a mortgage to finance the purchase of a home. Mortgages raise some important questions. How should the mortgage be treated in terms of determining your asset allocation? For investors with sufficient assets to have alternatives to using a large mortgage the questions are: Do I use my investment assets to keep the mortgage to a minimum or to pay down an existing mortgage, or do I borrow the maximum? As is often the case in investing, there is no right answer, just one right for each individual. Let's review the important issues that should be considered.

- A mortgage (or any other form of debt) should be considered as *negative* exposure to fixed-income assets and treated as such in the asset-allocation picture. For example, if you are holding a $200,000 mortgage and have $200,000 of fixed income assets, your fixed-income allocation is zero, not $200,000.
- It is unlikely an investor can beat the risk-free rate of return on a mortgage if the fixed-income asset is held in a tax-able account (unless interest rates have risen significantly

since the debt was incurred). If fixed income assets can be held in tax-advantaged accounts, depending on the investments chosen and assumed tax rate, borrowing might be advantageous.

- If a home is financed with a fixed-rate mortgage, the fixed rate provides inflation protection. A fixed-rate mortgage also has a feature enabling the borrower to prepay the loan if interest rates decline, usually without prepayment penalties: refinancing at a lower current rate. This provides protection against deflation and, for those with reinvestment risk, falling interest rates. If a home is financed with an adjustable-rate mortgage, the risk picture is considerably different, the rate moving up or down as interest rates change. Note that adjustable-rate mortgages do have annual and lifetime caps on the maximum amount the rates can adjust (up or down).

- Having little or no mortgage provides a high comfort level for investors. This is the "sleep well" issue. With little or no debt, investors are likely to be more comfortable accepting the risks inherent in equity investing and more likely to stay disciplined during the inevitable bear markets.

- With little or no debt, investors may feel more comfortable taking the greater risks inherent in value and small-cap stocks, allowing for higher expected returns within the equity allocation.

- From an investment portfolio standpoint, the principal reason to hold a mortgage is if the investor has a *high need to take risk* and estimates a large equity premium. The relatively low after-tax cost of the mortgage compared with the possibility of large relative returns from tax-efficient equity investing can make the mortgage an attractive alternative. As an example, assume a mortgage rate of 6 percent. The after-tax cost for a high-bracket individual is probably under 4 percent. On the other hand, an investor might expect his equity portfolio to return 10 percent and do so in a highly tax-efficient manner. That large differential can be tempting, but it means the assumption of all of the risks of equity investing.

The right answer ultimately comes down to the investor's marginal utility of wealth. The greater the marginal utility of wealth, the more equity one should hold (and thus have as big a mortgage as possible) and vice versa. Run the math before drawing any conclusion, including a Monte Carlo simulation as to asset allocation (see Chapter 16).

Prepay the Mortgage or Increase Tax-Advantaged Savings?

Many individuals are faced with the choice between either prepaying the mortgage or increasing their investments in tax-advantaged retirement accounts. The study, "Responsible Fools? The Trade-off Between Mortgage Prepayments and Tax-Deferred Retirement Savings," examines whether individuals were making financially optimal choices.[1]

The benefit of increasing the contribution to a tax-advantaged account is that the investment grows either on a tax-free basis (Roth account) or on a tax-deferred basis (IRA, 401(k), profit sharing). This allows for a tax arbitrage: mortgage interest is tax deductible if one itemizes, while earnings inside the retirement savings account are either tax deferred or tax free. That benefit more than offsets the slightly higher rate on the mortgage than can be earned by investing in a mortgage-backed security (MBS) of similar maturity. The advantage is enhanced by increasing the investment into a 401(k) plan if the individual also gains a matching contribution from the employer.

The authors concluded that almost 50 percent of individuals would be better off increasing contributions to retirement savings accounts rather than prepaying their mortgage. The individuals most likely to benefit are those in high tax brackets. The decision to increase retirement savings would yield incremental savings of between 11 cents on the dollar (if the investment is made in Treasury instruments); 17 if the investment is made in higher yielding MBS. The cumulative cost of inefficient decisions approaches $2 billion a year.

These benefits are basically riskless, a tax arbitrage. So, why do individuals forgo them? The authors hypothesized that a high aversion to debt—the desire to be debt free—can drive the "investment" choice toward paying down the mortgage instead of increasing retirement savings.

Three other points are worth noting. First, those with mortgages with a loan-to-value (LTV) of more than 80 percent should consider paying down the mortgage to that level, eliminating the cost of mortgage insurance. Second, the liquidity risk should be considered: Withdrawals from tax-advantaged accounts prior to the end of the early withdrawal period (prior to age 59½) face a 10-percent penalty. Of course, as you approach 59½ the risk of having to make an early withdrawal decreases. Third, if the money that would be invested in the tax-deferred accounts will be invested in low-yielding fixed income, it may make sense to pay down a mortgage. The mortgage rate might be so much higher than the fixed income yield that it swamps any tax arbitrage opportunities. As always, check current mortgage rates to see whether you can refinance at a lower interest rate.

Other Liabilities

Credit-card debt is generally the most expensive form of debt, and interest is not tax deductible. A good rule of thumb is that the first "investment" an individual should make is to pay it down, prior to any equity investing. Unless the debt is expected to be outstanding for a very short time, equities held in taxable accounts should be sold to pay off credit-card debt.

Nonsubsidized car loans and student loans are similar to credit-card debt, so the same rule of thumb generally applies. There may be cases where the loans are made at below-market rates, such as with car loans (when the price is discounted through the financing instead of lowering the price) or student loans. If the investor can earn a higher rate of return by investing in high-grade fixed-income securities, it doesn't make sense to pay down the debt early.

In most cases, we believe that individuals should not use margin to buy equities. With the cost of the margin being higher than the risk-free rate, equity investors using margin earn less than the market's required return on the margined asset. Part of the incremental risk is the risk of margin calls that might not be able to be met. Using margin for investing purposes is an inefficient use of one's capital, the rewards not commensurate with the risk. Only an investor with a very high marginal utility of wealth and a very high tolerance for risk should use margin to increase the equity allocation beyond 100 percent. As we discuss in Appendix A, there is a more prudent way to increase the expected return of the portfolio: Increase the exposure to the riskier asset classes of small-cap and value stocks. Higher expected returns fully compensate the investor for the incremental risk.

PART III

IMPLEMENTING THE PLAN

CHAPTER

8

Individual Securities or Mutual Funds

Once investors have decided on the appropriate asset allocation for their portfolio, they must decide on the best way to implement the plan. Investors have the choice of buying individual securities, mutual funds, or exchange-traded funds (ETFs). Mutual funds and ETFs often provide benefits over individual holdings, though those benefits may not exceed their associated expenses. The right answer will depend on a variety of issues unique to each investor or unique to the asset class to which the investor seeks exposure. We will examine the issue by looking at the benefits of each strategy, beginning with convenience.

Convenience

Unless the mutual fund is a load fund (which should be avoided because they add expenses without adding value) investors can buy and sell shares at the net asset value (NAV), where there is no bid-offer spread, and buying and selling is done at the same price. When the transaction is made directly with the fund sponsor it can generally be done without incurring any transactions costs. It also allows for the ease of reinvestment of dividends, distributions, and interest.

Another benefit of investing through mutual funds is the ability to trade relatively small amounts ($5,000 or $10,000) in order to generate cash for spending or in the portfolio rebalancing process. This may be especially important for bonds.

Diversification

The most important benefit of mutual funds is allowing investors to achieve broad diversification across an asset class at a lower cost than investors could do on their own. Broad diversification is important when the performance of a single security within the asset class has a relatively low correlation to the performance of the asset class itself. This is certainly the case with stocks.

For example, the performance of any one stock within the S&P 500 Index might be dramatically different than the performance of the entire index itself. The only way to ensure that you earn the return of the asset class is to own the entire asset class. There is a great deal of academic research on the subject of how much diversification is needed to keep tracking error—the variance between the performance of the entire asset class to the performance of a subset of the asset class—to an acceptable level. To keep it to an expected level of 5 percent (a level some investors would find unacceptably large), an investor would have to own approximately one hundred different individual stocks. And this is true only for the asset class of U.S. large-cap stocks. For asset classes such as small-cap stocks and international stocks a far greater number of individual stocks would be required. Building a globally diversified portfolio across eight to ten equity asset classes is well beyond the resources of almost all individual investors. Thus, mutual funds are the preferred choice when it comes to equities. The issue of diversification is quite different with fixed-income securities.

To begin with, investors limiting their holdings to Treasury securities have no need to diversify credit risk and can ensure themselves of wholesale prices by buying and selling via the Treasury direct program. In addition, there is a great deal of transparency of pricing of Treasury securities since prices are available on at least a daily basis in financial publications such as the *Wall Street Journal*. This helps keep pricing "honest." Since there is no evidence that managers are likely to add value by correctly forecasting interest rates and adjusting maturities accordingly, the only value a fund might add is convenience. That convenience can be purchased relatively cheaply through low cost vehicles like those offered by Vanguard or ETFs. Whether or not that cost is worth the convenience is an individual decision.

The diversification benefits funds provide becomes apparent once we move beyond the world of Treasuries. To evaluate the benefits of diversification, we must understand the source of the vast majority of returns of fixed-income assets.

Most returns of high-credit-quality, fixed-income securities are derived from interest-rate risk, which is the same for all securities, substantially reducing the benefits of and need for diversification. With U.S. government debt, the need for diversification is nonexistent: 100 percent of the risk is interest-rate risk that cannot be diversified away.

For bonds of the highest investment grades (securities of the U.S. Agencies and the Government Sponsored Enterprises) the need for diversification doesn't change much. There is little credit risk. With other AAA-rated bonds, especially AAA-rated municipal bonds, the need for diversification increases, but to a much lower degree than is the case with stocks. Think of bonds of the highest investment grades as commodities. Bonds of the same maturity and same high credit quality are good, but not perfect, substitutes for each other. While it would not be prudent to build a portfolio by selecting a small sample of stocks from one asset class, prudent diversification can be accomplished with a relatively small sample of very high credit quality bonds. The reason? You can have a high degree of confidence that the relatively small sample will produce returns similar to those produced by the entire population of similarly rated bonds of the same maturity. The higher the credit quality, the higher the confidence and less important any diversification. Conversely, the lower the credit quality, the more important the need for diversification of fixed-income assets. For example, junk bonds are not good substitutes for one another: Two junk bonds are far less likely to provide similar returns than two AAA-rated bonds. Investors seeking the higher *expected* returns that junk bonds provide should do so through a mutual fund owning several hundred different bonds.

Investors who limit themselves to bonds of the highest quality with a portfolio of perhaps $500,000 should consider building their own portfolio, saving mutual fund costs. A $500,000 portfolio allows investors to purchase securities in large enough blocks that they can limit the markups/downs to acceptable levels, diversifying the credit risk across perhaps as many as ten issuers. Owning that number of securities also allows for the diversification of maturity risk. This could be accomplished by buying one bond maturing in each of the next ten years.

Size Matters

Mutual funds buy and sells large blocks and so are able to minimize markups/downs and minimize trading costs. It is unlikely that individuals acting on their own can obtain institutional prices. Do-it-yourself investors with a $500,000 or larger portfolio should limit themselves to buying in the new-issue market where they can be assured they are getting institutional pricing. They should also only buy individual bonds if they are virtually certain they will be able to hold the bonds to maturity. An investor's trading costs for buying and selling in the secondary market could more than offset a fund's expense ratio. Individuals should avoid doing so on their own, unless they wish to make their broker rich.

Advantages of Individual Securities

While owning mutual funds provides advantages, there are advantages to owning individual securities. First, investors avoid operating expenses of the fund. Second, for taxable accounts, mutual fund investors can only tax loss harvest—have Uncle Sam share the pain—at the fund level. An investor owning individual bonds can manage taxes at the individual security level, providing more loss harvest opportunities. This is especially important with bond funds. Unlike equities, there are no fixed-income funds with the stated objective of tax managing their portfolios, harvesting losses along the way. In addition, while mutual funds can use realized losses, they cannot pass through to investors realized losses not offset by gains.

With Treasury bonds, where pricing is transparent and investors can deal directly with the Treasury, trading costs of tax loss harvesting would be low. When it comes to municipal and corporate bonds, investors trying to trade on their own would probably find any tax benefit from harvesting losses offset by the bid-offer spread, the dealer markdowns incurred when harvesting the losses, and the potential markup paid on the repurchase of a similar bond (unless the investor waited until a new issue was available).

Another benefit of owning individual bonds is that investors can take 100 percent control over the credit and maturity risks of their portfolio. This is generally not the case with mutual funds. They can also control the timing of cash flows from their portfolio. This is particularly important to investors relying on their fixed-income assets to provide the cash flow they need to maintain their desired lifestyle.

Separate Account Managers

Individual investors wishing to take advantage of the benefits of owning individual securities don't have to go it alone. They can use a separate account manager. A separate account manager builds a portfolio of individual securities tailored to the specific needs of the investor. The investor receives the benefits of owning individual securities without having to pay retail prices on transactions. The separate account manager should have access to the wholesale markets and be managing a large amount of assets to provide the maximum benefit to individual investors. We will examine why this is important.

A separate account manager can aggregate the purchases of different investors seeking to buy similar bonds. The following example will illustrate how investors can benefit from this process. A broker-dealer might offer to sell a block of $100,000 of a particular municipal or corporate bond at a price of 102. If the trade was for a block of $250,000, the offer might be just 101.75; for $500,000, 101.5. A firm that could aggregate five different purchases for $100,000 would be able to save each investor one-half of one percent on the trade. As long as each buyer was willing to be patient so that a "group" could be put together, each buyer would benefit from the aggregation process.

Separate account managers may be able to perform tax loss harvesting without incurring large trading costs. Assume a separate account manager has two investors both living in California. Each owns a $100,000 AAA-rated California municipal bond of similar maturity but from different issuers. Assume rates have risen significantly since the original purchases were made. Both investors would like to be able to harvest losses, but trading costs would be high. The manager/adviser simply contacts a broker-dealer and asks them to "cross" two trades. Investor A buys the bond of investor B, and investor B buys investor A's bond. The term "cross" implies that both purchases and sales are done at the same price, with no markup or markdown. Because broker-dealers take no risk in the transaction, they are willing to perform the service for a relatively low fee, perhaps $50 to $75. This is only possible if the manager/adviser has a large enough client base to make cross trades possible.

A good way to access a separate account manager is through a fee-only registered investment adviser (RIA) providing such services.

A small number of them provide investors with access to the wholesale markets. Although they won't add markups/downs to bond prices, service is not free: The investor pays for the value of the advice, typically an annual percentage of the total assets under management. However, the investor does avoid the fees of a money manager or mutual fund, helping offset the costs of the financial adviser's services. The adviser's value added services of fixed-income portfolio building and managing for taxes can be a bonus.

A Word of Caution

There is one more issue related to owning bond mutual funds (but not ETFs) of which investors should be both aware and concerned. Many bond funds, particularly closed-end funds that trade like stocks, use leverage in an attempt to increase returns. If they can borrow at a lower rate than the returns they earn, fund returns are enhanced. But leverage works both ways. In rising rate environments, its use can lead to outright losses. The use of leverage turns an investment into more of a speculation, a bet on interest rates. Funds employing leverage should be avoided.

Summary

The right answer on which approach is superior—individual securities or mutual funds (or ETFs)—depends on the unique situation of each investor, as well as how much they value convenience versus having to do it themselves.

If you are going to use mutual funds or ETFs, the following are our recommendations on selection criteria.

Fund Selection Criteria

Investors have more good choices available to them than ever before. Vanguard offers a broad array of low cost, passively managed funds. Low cost ETFs can also be excellent choices, especially for taxable accounts. Dimensional Fund Advisors (DFA) has, in our view, the best alternatives for passive asset class investing, especially for taxable accounts. However, DFA funds are only available through approved investment advisers and in some corporate retirement plans. When it comes to retirement plans offered by corporations, universities, and school districts, many investors have limited options. The choices are often between the lesser of evils (high expense, actively managed funds). With those factors in mind, the following suggestions are offered to help you decide which funds are the most appropriate. All else being equal:

- Choose the funds with the lowest expenses, recognizing that low expenses are not the only consideration. Some fund families are more successful at generating revenues from securities lending, thus increasing returns. DFA is particularly good at securities lending, often generating significantly more revenue than similar Vanguard funds or ETFs. This information can be found in a fund's prospectus.
- For taxable accounts, tax-managed funds should be the first choice, then ETFs.
- For value and small-cap allocations, choose the funds with the greatest exposure to the risk factors (highest weighted average BtM or lowest weighted average P/E ratio and smallest weighted average market capitalization). This will not only provide the purest exposure to the asset class (greater diversification benefits), but allow for a lower overall equity allocation (due to the greater expected returns).
- Funds with lower turnover should be preferred to funds with higher turnover. This is especially true for actively managed funds.
- Total market funds should be used to the extent possible as they reduce the need for, and costs of, rebalancing. For example, a total international fund that includes an allocation to emerging markets is preferable to separate allocations to developed markets and emerging markets. If your desired allocation to emerging markets is greater than the allocation in the total international fund, you can add a separate allocation to emerging markets, bringing the total allocation to your target.
- In addition to total market funds, DFA has a series of what they call "core" (multi-asset class) funds. They should be preferred to single-asset class funds, especially in taxable accounts.
- For taxable accounts, be aware that if a fund of funds (a fund whose holdings are other funds) is used, the foreign tax

credit will be lost. However, if more than half of the fund is invested in individual foreign securities and the remainder of the fund is structured as a fund of fund, the fund will qualify for a foreign tax credit (FTC). The market is continually evolving, with new and improved offerings. Stay on top of the latest in investment-fund "technology."

CHAPTER 9

Active versus Passive Management

For many investors, the active versus passive debate is the most contentious issue. We will present the evidence and hope you are convinced to follow our recommendation. However, the rest of the advice in this book applies regardless of which strategy you use to implement your investment plan.

There are two theories about investing. The conventional wisdom is that markets are inefficient. Smart people, through diligent efforts, can uncover which stocks the market has under or overvalued. This is called the art of stock selection. Smart people can also time the market, getting in ahead of the bull emerging into the arena and out ahead of the bear emerging from hibernation. This is called the art of market timing. Together, stock selection and market timing make up the art of active management.

The other theory is that markets are efficient, that the price of a security is the best estimate of the correct price: otherwise, the market would clear at a different price. If markets are efficient, and accounting for the expense of the effort, attempts to outperform it are highly unlikely to prove productive.

The debate about which strategy is the one most likely to produce the best results is the financial equivalent of the "Tastes great! Less filling!" debate. Like that debate, it is unlikely to end. While it rages, we can examine the evidence from academic studies, allowing you to make an informed decision on which strategy to adopt.

The Evidence

If the markets are inefficient, we should see evidence of the *persistent* ability to outperform appropriate *risk-adjusted* benchmarks. And that persistence should be greater than randomly expected. We can test which theory the historical evidence supports by reviewing the literature on the performance of mutual funds, pension plans, and individual investors. The evidence on hedge funds and private equity was covered in Chapter 6.

Mutual Funds

Mark Carhart's 1997 study, "On Persistence in Mutual-fund Performance," analyzed the performance of 1,892 mutual funds for the period 1961–93. The following is a summary of his findings:

- The average actively managed fund underperformed its appropriate passive benchmark on a pretax basis by about 1.8 percent per annum.
- There is no persistence in performance beyond that which would be randomly expected. Past performance of active managers is a very poor predictor of their future performance.[1]

Russ Wermers found even worse results in his 2000 study, "Mutual-fund performance: An Empirical Decomposition into Stock-Picking Talent, Style, Transaction Costs, and Expenses." The study covered the twenty-year period from 1975–94 and included a universe of 1,788 funds in existence during the period. He found the average underperformance on a risk-adjusted basis was 2.2 percent per annum.[2]

Pension Plans

If anyone could beat the market, it should be the pension plans of U.S. companies. First, pension plans control large sums of money. They have access to the best and brightest portfolio managers, each clamoring to manage the billions of dollars in these plans (and earn large fees). Pension plans can also invest with managers most individuals don't have access to, having insufficient assets to meet the minimums of these superstar managers.

Second, these pension plans hire managers with track records of outperforming their benchmarks, or at least matching them. They never hire managers with records of underperformance.

Third, they hire managers who make wonderful presentations, explaining in great detail and with polished PowerPoints why they have succeeded and will continue to succeed.

Fourth, many, if not the majority, of these pension plans hire professional consultants (Frank Russell, SEI, and Goldman Sachs) to help them perform due diligence in interviewing, screening, and ultimately selecting the very best of the best. Frank Russell has boasted they have over seventy analysts performing over two thousand interviews a year. You can be sure these consultants have thought of every conceivable screen to find the best fund managers. They considered performance records, management tenure, depth of staff, consistency of performance (to ensure a long-term record is not the result of one or two lucky years), performance in bear markets, consistency of implementation of strategy, turnover, and costs. It is unlikely there is something you or your financial adviser would think of that they had not already considered.

Fifth, as individuals, it is rare that we would have the luxury of personally interviewing money managers and performing as thorough a due diligence. And we generally don't have professionals helping us avoid mistakes in the process.

With those five key points in mind, we examine the evidence.

There are two major studies on the performance of pension plans. The first is Rob Bauer, Rik Frehen, Hurber Lum, and Roger Otten's 2007 study, "The Performance of U.S. Pension Plans." The study covered 716 defined benefit plans (1992–2004) and 238 defined contribution plans (1997–2004). The authors found that returns relative to benchmarks were close to zero and that there was no persistence in pension-plan performance. Importantly, they also found that neither fund size, degree of outsourcing, nor company stock holdings were factors driving performance. This finding refutes the claim that large pension plans are handicapped by their size. Small plans did no better. The authors concluded: "The striking similarities in performance patterns over time makes skill differences highly unlikely."[3]

The second study, Amit Goyal and Sunil Wahal's 2008 "The Selection and Termination of Investment Management Firms by

Plan Sponsors," appearing in the *Journal of Finance*,[4] examined the selection and termination of investment management firms by plan sponsors: public and corporate pension plans, unions, foundations, and endowments. The study covered the hiring and firing decisions of 3,700 plan sponsors from 1994 to 2003, finding:

- Plan sponsors hire investment managers with large positive excess returns up to three years prior to hiring.
- The return chasing behavior does not deliver positive excess returns thereafter.
- Post-hiring excess returns are indistinguishable from zero.
- If plan sponsors had stayed with the fired investment managers, their returns would have been larger than those actually delivered by the newly hired managers.

These results did not include any trading costs that would have accompanied transitioning a portfolio from one manager's holdings to the holdings preferred by the new manager. In other words, all the activity was counterproductive.

Individual Investors

Brad Barber, professor of finance at the University of California, Davis, and Terrance Odean, associate professor of finance at the University of California, Berkeley, have done a series of studies on the performance of individual investors, concluding they aren't as bad at stock picking as many people think. They are worse. Their findings:

- The stocks that individual investors buy *trail* the overall market, and the stocks that they sell *beat* the market after the sale. This result did not even consider transactions costs or tax implications of an active trading strategy.[5]
- The more investors traded, the worse the results. Those trading the most underperform a market index by over 5 percent per annum. On a risk-adjusted basis the underperformance increases to 10 percent per annum.[6]
- Proving more heads are not better than one, investment clubs trailed a broad market index by almost 4 percent per annum, and by more than that on a risk-adjusted basis.[7]

The Search for the Holy Grail: Why Is Persistent Outperformance So Hard to Find?

While it is easy to identify money managers with great performance *after the fact,* as we have seen, there is no evidence of the ability to do this *before the fact.*

The efficient markets hypothesis (EMH) tells us that lack of persistence should be expected: It is only by random good luck that a fund is able to persistently outperform after the expenses of its efforts. There is also a practical reason for the lack of persistence: Successful active management sows the seeds of its own destruction.

Jonathan Berk, a professor at the University of California, Berkeley, suggested the following thought process:

> Who gets money to manage? Well, since investors know who the skilled managers are, money will flow to the best manager first. Eventually, this manager will receive so much money that it will impact his ability to generate superior returns and his expected return will be driven down to the second-best manager's expected return. At that point, investors will be indifferent to investing with either manager and so funds will flow to both managers until their expected returns are driven down to the third-best manager. This process will continue until the expected return of investing with any manager is the benchmark expected return: the return investors can expect to receive by investing in a passive strategy of similar riskiness. At that point, investors are indifferent between investing with active managers or just indexing, and an equilibrium is achieved.[8]

Berk pointed out that the manager with the most skill ends up with the most money, adding: "When capital is supplied competitively by investors but ability is scarce only participants with the skill in short supply can earn economic rents. Investors who choose to invest with active managers cannot expect to receive positive excess returns on a risk-adjusted basis. If they did, there would be an excess supply of capital to those managers."[9]

This is an important insight. Just as the EMH explains why investors cannot use publicly available information to beat the market (because all investors have access to that information, and it is, therefore, already imbedded in prices), the same is true of active managers. Investors should not expect to outperform the market by using publicly available information to select active managers. Any excess return will go to the active manager, in the form of higher expenses.

The process is simple. Investors observe benchmark-beating performance and funds flow into the top performers. The investment inflow eliminates return persistence because fund managers face diminishing returns to scale.

Edelen, Evans, and Kadlec's 2007 study "Scale Effects in Mutual Fund Performance: The Role of Trading Costs," provides evidence supporting Berk's theory. The authors examined the role of trading costs as a source of diseconomies of scale for mutual funds. They studied the annual trading costs for 1,706 U.S. equity funds during the period 1995–2005, finding:

- Trading costs for mutual funds are on average greater in magnitude than the expense ratio.
- The variation in returns is related to fund trade size.
- Annual trading costs bear a statistically significant negative relation to performance.
- Trading has an increasingly detrimental impact on performance as a fund's relative trade size increases.
- Trading fails to recover its costs: $1 in trading costs reduced fund assets by $0.41. While trading does not adversely impact performance at funds with a relatively small average trade size, trading costs *decrease* fund assets by roughly $0.80 for relatively large trade size funds.
- Flow-driven trades are shown to be significantly more costly than discretionary trades. Flow-driven trades are those created by investors' additions to and withdrawals from a fund. This nondiscretionary trade motive partially—but not fully—explains the negative impact of trading on performance.
- Relative trade size subsumes fund size in regressions of fund returns. Thus, trading costs are likely to be the primary source of diseconomies of scale for funds.

The authors concluded: "Our evidence directly establishes scale effects in trading as a source of diminishing returns to scale from active management."[10]

There is another reason why successful active management sows the seeds of its own destruction. As a fund's assets increase, either trading costs will rise, or the fund will have to diversify across more securities to limit those costs. However, the more a fund diversifies, the more it looks and performs like its benchmark index. It becomes what is known as a *closet index* fund. If it chooses this alternative, its higher total costs have to be spread across a smaller amount of differentiated holdings, increasing the hurdle of outperformance.

For example, let's assume an active fund has an expense ratio of 1.2 percent, its benchmark index fund an expense ratio of 0.2 percent, and 90 percent of the active funds holdings are the same as those of the index fund. Those 90 percent of assets cannot outperform the index. Thus, the 10 percent of the active fund's assets that are different from the index fund must do all the heavy lifting to overcome the cost differential for 100 percent of assets. This is a very tall order, indeed.

The Value of Economic Forecasts

There is another reason why it is so difficult to persistently beat the market without taking more risk: The underlying basis for most stock market forecasts is an economic forecast. Do these forecasts have any value?

In 1985 William Sherden, preparing testimony as an expert witness, analyzed the track records of inflation projections by different economic forecasting methods. He compared those forecasts to the "naive" forecast: projecting today's inflation rate into the future. To his surprise (since he was a so-called expert), he found the naive forecast to be the most accurate. That led Sherden to review economic forecasts made during the period 1970–95. One finding was that economists could not predict the important turning points in the economy. Of forty-eight predictions, forty-six missed the turning points in the economy. He also found that even economists who directly or indirectly can influence the economy—the Federal Reserve, the Council of Economic Advisers, and the Congressional Budget Office—had forecasting records worse than pure chance. He concluded there are no economic forecasters who consistently lead the pack in forecasting accuracy. Even consensus forecasts did not improve accuracy.

Sherden also studied the performance of seven forecasting professions: investment experts, meteorology, technology assessment, demography, futurology, organizational planning, and economics. While none of the experts were very expert, the folks most often joked about (meteorologists) had the best predictive powers. Sherden also made this important observation:

> Despite recent innovations in information technology and decades of academic research, successful stock market prediction has remained an elusive goal. In fact, the market is getting more complex and unpredictable as global trading brings in many new investors from numerous countries, computerized exchanges speed up transactions, and investors think up clever schemes to try to beat the market. Overall, we have not made progress in predicting the stock market, but this has not stopped the investment business from continuing the quest, and making $100 billion annually doing so.

Sherden used his research to write his book *The Fortune Sellers.*[11]

Even professional economic forecasters have acknowledged the difficult hurdles economists face. Consider this admission from Michael Evans, the founder of Chase Econometrics: "The problem with macro [economic] forecasting is that no one can do it."[12] And this is from the head of a firm that sells economic forecasts.

The Value of Security Analysis

There is one last example you should consider: just how difficult a task it is to outperform the collective wisdom of the market.

In May 1999, at a conference of financial economists at UCLA's Anderson School of Business, Bradford Cornell used Intel Corporation in a case study that provides insights into the value of security analysts. As you will see, because much of the value of companies with high growth rates comes from distant cash flows, the value of their stock is highly sensitive to the size of the equity risk premium (ERP): the risk premium above the rate on riskless Treasury instruments investors demand for accepting the risks of equity ownership. In 1999, Intel was certainly considered a company with expectations for a high rate of growth.

Intel had accumulated over $10 billion in cash. The Board of Directors was trying to determine if it made sense to use a substantial portion of the cash to repurchase its stock. At the time, the stock was trading at about $120 per share. Based on publicly available forecasts of future cash flows, Cornell demonstrated that if the ERP were 3 percent, Intel's stock would be worth $204. If the ERP were 5 percent, the stock would be worth $130 (about the current price). And if the ERP were 7.2 percent, the stock would be worth just $82.

Buy, Sell, or Hold?

With such a wide range of estimated values, what should the board do? If the stock was worth $204, they should begin an aggressive repurchase program. If it was worth $82, they should take advantage of the current "overvaluation" and raise capital by issuing more shares.

The board was faced with two problems. The first was that the valuations assumed that cash-flow projections were *known*. Not even the board, let alone some security analyst, can see the future with such clarity. In the real world, we can only estimate future cash flows. The second problem: Why would the board believe it could predict the ERP better than the market could?

If corporate insiders have such great difficulty in determining a "correct" valuation, even with greater access to information than any security analyst, it is easy to understand why the results of active management are so poor and inconsistent.

The Tyrannical Nature of an Efficient Market

One of the fundamental tenets of the EMH is that in a competitive financial environment successful trading strategies self-destruct by being self-limiting. When discovered, they are eliminated by the very act of exploiting the strategy. Economics professors Dwight Lee and James Verbrugge of the University of Georgia explain the power of the efficient markets theory in the following manner:

> The efficient markets theory is practically alone among theories in that it becomes more powerful when people discover serious inconsistencies between it and the real world. If a clear efficient market anomaly is discovered, the behavior (or lack

of behavior) that gives rise to it will tend to be eliminated by competition among investors for higher returns. . . . If stock prices are found to follow predictable seasonal patterns this knowledge will elicit responses that have the effect of eliminating the very patterns that they were designed to exploit. The implication is striking. The more empirical flaws that are discovered in the efficient markets theory the more robust the theory becomes. . . . Those who do the most to ensure that the efficient market theory remains fundamental to our understanding of financial economics are not its intellectual defenders, but those mounting the most serious empirical assault against it.[13]

In summary, while the markets may not be perfectly efficient, the prudent investment strategy is to behave as if they were.

This evidence convinced us that the winning strategy is to adopt a passive investment strategy. It convinced the American Law Institute, as well.

The Prudent Investor Rule

In May 1992, the American Law Institute rewrote the Prudent Investor Rule. Here is some of what the institute had to say in doing so:

- The restatement's objective is to liberate expert trustees to pursue challenging, rewarding, non-traditional strategies and to provide other trustees with clear guidance to safe harbors that are practical and expectedly rewarding.
- Investing in index funds is a passive but practical investment alternative.
- Risk may be reduced by mixing risky assets with essentially riskless assets, rather than creating an entirely low-risk portfolio.
- *Active strategies entail investigation and expenses that increase transaction costs, including capital gains taxation.* Proceeding with such a program involves judgments by the trustee that gains from the course of action in question can reasonably be expected to *compensate for additional cost and risks,* and the course of action to be *undertaken is reasonable in terms of its economic rationale.*

The American Law Institute recognized both the significance and efficacy of modern portfolio theory (MPT) and that active management delivers inconsistent and poor results. The institute had the following to say about market efficiency:

- Economic evidence shows that the major capital markets of this country are *highly efficient,* in the sense available information is rapidly digested and reflected in market prices.
- Fiduciaries and other investors are confronted with potent evidence that the application of expertise, investigation, and diligence in efforts to "beat the market" ordinarily promises little or no payoff, or even a negative payoff after taking account of research and transaction costs.
- Empirical research supporting the theory of efficient markets reveals that in such markets, skilled professionals have rarely been able to identify underpriced securities with any regularity.
- Evidence shows little correlation between fund managers' earlier successes and their ability to produce above-market returns in subsequent periods.

The Uniform Prudent Investor Act is currently the law in the vast majority of states. It sets forth standards that govern the investment activities of trustees. And it adopts MPT as the standard by which fiduciaries invest funds.

The Benefits of Passive Investing

The goal of a passive-investment strategy is to capture the returns of markets. The use of passive investment vehicles will provide you with the following benefits:

- **Broad diversification within each asset class.** Passively managed funds will typically own far more securities than similar (the same asset class) actively managed ones. This serves to eliminate, or at least minimize, unsystematic risk: risk for which investors are not compensated because it can be diversified away.
- **Low fund expense ratios.** Passively managed funds typically have much lower expense ratios than actively managed ones.

- **Low turnover.** This provides two benefits. First, the fund will experience lower trading costs, both from the bid/offer spread incurred when trading and also from what is known as market impact costs. Market impact occurs when a mutual fund or other investor wants to buy or sell a large block of stock. The fund's purchases or sales will cause the stock to move beyond its current bid (lower) or offer (higher) price, increasing the cost of trading. While you don't receive a bill for these expenses, they do lower returns. Second, for taxable accounts, there is the burden of capital gains taxes created by turnover. Lower turnover translates into greater tax efficiency.
- **Control over the portfolio's asset allocation.** The charters of most actively managed mutual funds give their portfolio managers the discretionary freedom to shift their allocations between asset classes. This can cause investors to both lose control of their asset allocation decisions and take unintended risks by unknowingly investing in markets, or types of instruments, they wanted to avoid.

Summary

Wall Street needs and wants you to play the game of active investing. They know your odds of outperforming appropriate benchmarks are so low that it is not in your interest to play. They need you to play so that *they* (not you) make the most money. They make it by charging high fees for active management that persistently delivers poor performance. The financial media also want and need you to play so that you "tune in." That is how *they* (not you) make money.

If you are not yet convinced, consider the following admission by Steve Galbraith. Galbraith teaches security analysis at Columbia University in its M.B.A. program. He is a limited partner at Maverick Capital and the former Chief U.S. Investment Strategist at Morgan Stanley. He also co-authored Morgan Stanley's US Economic Perspectives. In March 2002, Galbraith invited John Bogle, the founder and former chairman of the Vanguard Group and a strong advocate of passive investing, to speak to his class.

In a letter to investors in the April 3, 2002, issue, Galbraith related the following about Bogle's presentation.

"He laid out the case against active management and for indexing quite powerfully. My guess is that more than a few students left the class wondering just what the heck their hard-earned tuition dollars were doing going to a class devoted to the seemingly impossible—analyzing securities to achieve better-than-market returns. . . . At least the students have the excuse of being early in their careers; what's mine for staying the course in my current role?" He also admitted: "*We recognize that the odds are against active managers.*"

Galbraith pointed out that actual returns to investors in the greatest bull market ever ranged "from the subprime to the ridiculous." Galbraith closed his letter on a very revealing note: "From our perspective, *perhaps in a triumph of hope over experience,* we continue to believe active managers can add value." Given the role of his employer, to believe otherwise would be committing professional suicide. The winning strategy for investors is simply to accept market returns. Unfortunately, that is not the winning strategy for Morgan Stanley and its profits.

You don't have to play the game of active management. Instead, you can earn market (not average) rates of return with low expenses and high tax efficiency. You can do so by investing in passively managed investment vehicles like index funds and passive asset class funds. You are virtually guaranteed to outperform the majority of both professionals and individual investors. You win by not playing.

If you do decide to invest in actively managed funds, you will, as Galbraith noted, have the hope of outperformance. Unfortunately, the evidence demonstrates that odds of success are so low it is imprudent to try. It is the triumph of hype, hope, and marketing over wisdom and experience.

CHAPTER 10

The Asset Location Decision

When faced with a choice of locating assets in either taxable or tax-advantaged accounts, taxable investors should have a *preference* for holding equities (versus fixed-income investments) in taxable accounts. But regardless of whether they hold stocks or fixed-income investments, investors should always prefer to first fund their Roth IRA or deductible retirement accounts (IRA, 401k or 403b) before investing any taxable dollars. Because tax-advantaged accounts are the most tax-efficient investment accounts, investors should always take maximum advantage of their ability to fund them. The one exception is the need to provide liquidity for unanticipated funding requirements.

There are six advantages to holding equities rather than fixed income in a taxable account:

- Equities receive capital gains treatment while fixed-income investments are taxed at ordinary income tax rates. At least as of this writing, qualified dividends are taxed at a preferential rate.
- Securities in taxable accounts receive a step-up in basis for the heirs at death, eliminating capital gains taxes, though not the estate tax. On the downside, securities with unrealized losses in taxable accounts receive a step-down in basis at death—a good reason to harvest losses when available.
- Capital gains taxes are due only when realized. Investors have some ability to time the realization of gains. In addition, the

advent of core funds, tax-managed funds, and exchanged-traded funds (ETFs) has greatly improved the tax efficiency of equity investing.

- When there are losses in taxable accounts, the losses can be harvested for tax purposes. The more volatile the asset, the more valuable the option to harvest losses. Equities are more volatile than fixed-income assets.

- Assets held in taxable accounts can be donated to charities. By donating the appreciated shares (the preference should be to donate the shares with the largest long-term capital gain), capital gains taxes can be avoided. Because equities have higher expected returns than fixed income assets, this option is more valuable for equities.

- Taxes on dividends of foreign stock holdings are often withheld at the source. Investors can, however, claim a foreign tax credit (FTC) that can then be used as a credit against U.S. taxes. This credit is lost if the asset is held in a tax-advantaged account. Currently, the loss of the FTC leads to a reduction of returns of about 9 percent of the amount of the dividend. This figure can change over time and across funds due to changes in withholding rates, tax treaties, and asset allocation within a fund. Remember that if the investment in international assets is a "fund of funds" structure, no portion of the FTC can be passed on to the investor by the fund of funds. However, if more than half of the fund is invested in individual foreign securities and the remainder structured as a fund of fund, the fund will qualify for a FTC.

Exceptions

The strategy of preferring to hold equities in taxable accounts and fixed-income investments in tax-advantaged accounts has some exceptions:

- **REITs:** Because their dividends are considered nonqualified (and, therefore, taxed at ordinary income-tax rates), real estate investment trusts (REITs) are a tax-inefficient equity asset class. In addition, the majority of the return on REITs is in the form of dividends, not capital gains. Since investors can hold tax-efficient municipal bonds in taxable accounts, those

investors that value the diversification benefits of REITs should locate the REIT holdings in a tax-advantaged account.
- **CCF:** Those investors who value the diversification benefit of a common contractual fund (CCF) should locate these assets in tax-advantaged accounts, even if that means holding fixed-income investments in taxable accounts. Again, tax-efficient municipal bonds can be held in taxable accounts.

Order of Preference

The asset allocation for some investors will require their holding equities in both taxable and tax-advantaged accounts. Here is the order of preference for holding assets in a tax-advantaged account:

1. REITs and CCF
2. TIPS
3. Nominal bonds
4. Domestic equities—value
5. Domestic equities—small-cap
6. Emerging markets—value
7. Emerging markets—small-cap
8. Emerging markets—total market/core
9. International equities—small-cap
10. International equities—value
11. Domestic equities—total market/core
12. Domestic equities—large-cap
13. International equities—total market/core

The order of preference may be different for investors with access to tax-managed funds, such as those of Vanguard and Dimensional Fund Advisors. Because of their high degree of tax efficiency, they are the preferred choice for taxable accounts. ETFs can also be highly tax efficient: Their availability can also impact the pecking order.

Additional Considerations

Consider these additional points:

- The more tax-efficient funds should be placed in the taxable accounts.

- Tax-managed funds will generally be more tax efficient than funds not managed for tax efficiency.
- The broader the definition of the asset class, the more tax efficient the fund is likely to be. For example, a total market fund will be more tax efficient than a narrow asset class fund, such as a small-cap fund. A small-cap fund that holds both value and growth will be more tax efficient than a small-cap value fund.
- Large-cap funds are more tax efficient than small-cap funds.
- Marketwide and growth funds are more tax efficient than value funds.
- Multiple asset class funds (such as core funds and total stock market funds) are more tax efficient than single asset class funds due to lower turnover as stocks "migrate" from one asset class to another. For example, an international core fund holding both developed and emerging markets will be more tax efficient than one holding two separate funds. In addition to the reduction in forced turnover, rebalancing costs between individual asset classes will be reduced, and the core funds will not have to trade if a country is reclassified from an emerging market to a developed one.
- The more volatile the asset class, the more valuable the tax option—the ability to harvest losses.
- Because not all foreign dividends qualify for the lower tax rate applicable to qualified dividends, the amount of unqualified dividends a fund distributes should be considered.

Application. An investor has a total portfolio of $2 million: $1 million in a taxable account and $1 million in a tax-advantaged account. First, determine the appropriate asset allocation based on the investor's ability, willingness, and need to take risk. Assume it is 54 percent stocks, 3 percent REITs, 3 percent CCF, and 40 percent bonds.

Step One: Locate 3 percent ($60,000) allocations to both REITs and CCF, for a total of $120,000 to the tax-advantaged accounts. That leaves $880,000 yet to be allocated to the tax-advantaged accounts.

Step Two: Place the 40 percent of bonds ($800,000) in the tax-advantaged accounts. That leaves $80,000 of equities that can be held in the tax-advantaged accounts. Place the least tax efficient equities in the tax-advantaged account.

Advanced Concept

There is an alternative strategy to consider: Since fixed income is more attractive if you have a tax-advantaged account, you might consider maximizing that benefit by purchasing even more bonds in the tax-advantaged account. To accomplish this objective without lowering the expected return (need to take risk), lower the equity allocation (which lowers the expected return of the portfolio) and raise the exposure to the size and value risk premiums, thus restoring the portfolio's expected return to its original level. This both improves the portfolio's tax efficiency and reduces the potential dispersion of returns. You are trading off a lower opportunity for outstanding returns (a reduction in the size of the good fat right tail of potential distributions) in exchange for a lower risk of the potential for extremely negative results (a reduction in the size of the bad left fat tail of potential distributions). One potential negative: You increase tracking-error risk. (See Appendix A for further discussion of this strategy).

Balanced and Lifestyle Funds

One mutual fund product that has proliferated in recent years, especially inside corporate retirement and profit-sharing plans, is the balanced, or lifestyle fund. The idea of the product is fundamentally sound: Create a fund of funds that invests in various asset classes. These funds can be structured to accommodate investors covering the full spectrum from aggressive (100 percent equity allocation) to very conservative (20 percent equity allocation). They provide the following benefits:

- They allow investors to hold in one fund a diversified portfolio that can include exposure to both U.S. equities (large growth, large value, small, and small value) and international ones (international large and possibly including emerging markets).
- They automatically rebalance to targeted exposures, providing discipline.
- If the fund is not an all-equity fund, it will also rebalance between equities and fixed income, once again providing discipline.

However, there are some important negative features:

- For investors with a choice of location (unless the fund is all-equity), combining equities and fixed income assets in one fund results in the investor holding one of the two assets in a tax-inefficient manner. If the fund of funds is held in a taxable account, the investor is holding the fixed-income assets in a tax-inefficient location. If the fund is held in a tax-advantaged account, the equities are being held in a tax-inefficient location.
- If the fund is held in a taxable account the investor loses the ability to loss harvest at the individual asset class level.
- If the fund is in a tax-advantaged account, the investor loses the ability to use any foreign tax credits generated by the international equity holdings. Even in a taxable account, as a fund of funds, the investor loses the ability to use the foreign tax credit.
- If the fund is held in a taxable account the equities should be in tax-managed funds. We are not aware of any lifestyle or balanced fund that tax-manages the equity portion. This makes sense, since the fund does not know in which location it will be held. Finally, if the fund is held in a taxable account it is likely that the fixed-income portion should be in municipal bonds. Otherwise, there is a loss of tax efficiency.

Individually, these important negative features impact the after-tax return of the fund. Collectively, they can be very damaging. The bottom line is this: if the use of a balanced or lifestyle fund leads to an inefficient choice of location, its use should be avoided unless the investor is in a relatively low tax bracket.

CHAPTER

11

The Care and Maintenance
of the Portfolio

Think of your portfolio like a garden: To keep it producing the desired results, it needs disciplined care, weeding, and nourishing. Your investment portfolio also requires regular maintenance to control the most important determinant of risk and returns: the portfolio's asset allocation. You maintain control through rebalancing and tax management.

Rebalancing

Rebalancing a portfolio means minimizing or eliminating its "style drift," caused by market movement. Style drift causes the risk and expected return of the portfolio to change.

There are some myths about rebalancing, the first being that rebalancing is a "reversion to the mean" strategy. This is false: Consider a portfolio with an asset allocation of 50 percent stocks/ 50 percent bonds. Stocks have returned 10 percent and are expected to return 10 percent while bonds have returned 6 percent and are expected to return 6 percent. The first year, stocks return 9 percent and bonds 7 percent. A strategy based on reversion to the mean of returns would sell bonds (since they produced above-average returns) to buy stocks (since they produced below-average returns). However, since the portfolio would then have an asset allocation of greater than 50 percent for stocks, rebalancing would require stocks be sold to buy more bonds, or buying sufficient bonds to increase the bond allocation to 50 percent.

The second myth about rebalancing is that it increases returns. That will not be the case most of the time. Most of the time rebalancing will require investors sell some of the higher expected returning asset class to purchase more of the lower expected returning asset class. For example, we would usually expect to have to sell stocks to buy fixed income assets. Similarly, we should expect we will mostly have to sell value stocks to buy growth stocks, small stocks to buy large stocks, and/or emerging market stocks to buy developed market stocks. In each case, we will be selling the higher expected returning asset class to buy the lower expected returning asset class. While achieving the objective of restoring the portfolio's risk profile, in each of these cases rebalancing lowers the expected return of the portfolio. This will not always be true. When bonds outperform stocks, rebalancing will increase the expected return of the portfolio, as you reduce the allocation of the lower expected returning asset class to increase the allocation of the higher expected returning asset class.

The Rebalancing Table

Your IPS should include an asset allocation and rebalancing table. The table should include both the target levels for each asset class and the minimum and maximum levels to which the allocations will be allowed to drift. Some drift should be allowed to occur: Rebalancing generally involves costs, including transactions fees and taxes in taxable accounts.

We suggest using a 5/25 percent rule in an asset class's allocation before considering rebalancing. In other words, consider rebalancing if the change in an asset class's allocation is greater than either an absolute 5 percent or 25 percent of the original percentage allocation. The actual percentages used are not as important as having a specific plan and the discipline to adhere to the plan. In your own situation, a 4/20 rule might be as appropriate as a 5/25 rule.

Application of 5/25 Rule: Assume that an asset class was given an allocation of 10 percent. Applying the 5 percent rule, one would rebalance only when that asset class's allocation had either risen to 15 percent (10 percent + 5 percent) or fallen to 5 percent

(10 percent – 5 percent). Using the 25 percent rule, however, one would reallocate if the asset class had risen or fallen by just 2.5 percent (10 percent × 25 percent) to either 12.5 percent (10 percent + 2.5 percent) or 7.5 percent (10 percent – 2.5 percent). In this case, the 25 percent figure is the governing factor. If one had a 50 percent asset class allocation, the 5/25 percent rule would make the 5 percent figure the governing factor, since 5 percent is less than 25 percent of 50 percent (12.5 percent). So, one rebalances if either the 5 percent or 25 percent test indicates such a need.

The need for rebalancing should be checked at three levels.

- The broad level of equities and fixed income;
- The level of domestic and international asset classes;
- The more narrowly defined individual asset class level, such as emerging markets, real estate, small-cap and value.

A sample asset allocation and rebalancing table is shown in Chapter 2.

The Rebalancing Process

There are two ways to rebalance. The first is to sell one or more funds to raise sufficient cash to purchase the appropriate amount of one or more other funds. The other way is to use new cash to raise the allocations of the asset classes that are below targeted levels. A combination of the two strategies can be used. Using new cash is preferred, as it reduces transactions costs and for taxable accounts reduces/eliminates the generation of capital gains. Whenever new cash is available for investment purposes it should be used to rebalance the portfolio.

One strategy that can be employed is having distributions paid in cash rather than automatically reinvested, using that cash to rebalance. When making this decision, consider the size of the portfolio and size of the transactions costs. For small accounts, where transactions costs are present, this might not be a good strategy. Here are some other recommendations on the rebalancing process.

- If rebalancing is required, consider whether incremental funds will become available in the near future, such as a tax refund, a bonus, or proceeds from a sale. If capital gains taxes will be generated by rebalancing, it might be prudent to wait until the new cash is available.

- Consider delaying rebalancing if it generates significant short-term capital gains. The size of the gain should be a major consideration: The larger the gain, the greater the benefit of waiting until long-term-gains treatment can be obtained. Another consideration: How long before additional funds can be generated to rebalance?
- If significant capital gains taxes are generated, consider rebalancing only to the minimum/maximum tolerance ranges, rather than restoring allocations to the target levels.

Rebalancing may generate capital-gains taxes. Whenever possible, rebalance with new investment dollars or using tax-advantaged accounts.

Tax Management Strategies

In managing the portfolio for tax efficiency, the most important decisions are at the beginning: making sure asset location decisions are made correctly, and using the most tax-efficient vehicles, such as core and tax-managed funds. There are other important strategies.

Tax Loss Harvesting

Tax management is a year-round job. Far too many investors wait until the end of the calendar year to check for opportunities to harvest losses. These should be checked for throughout the year.

A loss should be harvested whenever the value of tax deduction significantly exceeds the transactions cost of the trades required to harvest the loss, immediately reinvesting the proceeds in a manner avoiding the wash sale rule (see Glossary). Waiting until the end of the year is a mistake: Losses that might exist early in the year may no longer exist. In addition, it can be important to realize any short-term losses before they become long term. Short-term losses are first deducted against short-term gains that would otherwise be taxed at the higher ordinary income tax rates. Long-term losses are first deducted against long-term gains that would otherwise be taxed at the lower capital gains rate.

For example, before any loss harvesting, imagine a taxpayer has *realized* short- and long-term gains and *unrealized* short-term losses. These losses can be harvested, reducing the short-term gain that would have otherwise been taxed at higher ordinary tax rates. If not harvested until they became long-term losses, they would reduce long-term gains that would have been taxed at the lower long-term capital gains rate.

The Mechanics of Harvesting

Investors who tax-loss harvest reset their cost basis to a new, lower level. The tax-rate differential then provides the opportunity to arbitrage the tax system. Here is how such arbitrage might work.

On January 1, 2009, you invest $10,000 in a fund. On March 1, 2009, the value of the fund has shrunk to $7,000. You sell the fund. Since the fund was held for less than one year, the loss is characterized as short term. Assuming a 35 percent ordinary federal income tax rate, you will have a $1,050 tax savings, leaving a net economic loss of $1,950.

Note that the deduction of capital losses in excess of capital gains is limited to a deduction against $3,000 of other income, though losses can be carried forward indefinitely during a taxpayer's lifetime. If there are net long-term gains in a given year, any net short-term losses not already used to offset short-term gains must be applied against those long-term gains, reducing the value of the deduction to that of the lower long-term capital gains rate.

Since you don't wish to be out of the market for thirty days, the time needed to avoid the "wash sale" rule, you use the $7,000 of sale proceeds to immediately purchase a similar fund. For example, if you had sold a Total Stock Market Fund, you might purchase a Russell 1000 Fund. Since they would be similar in their exposures to the three risk factors (market, size, and value) they have similar expected returns.

Continuing the example, jump forward to March 2, 2010 (one year and a day). Both the fund you sold and the one you purchased have each risen to $10,000. If you had simply held the first fund, you would have had neither gain nor loss, and no tax benefit in the prior year. If, however, you harvested the loss, replaced the original fund with the similar fund, and then sold it on March 2, 2010 (to repurchase the preferred holding), you would have a gain of

$3,000 on which you would pay taxes at the long-term capital gains rate. Assume it is 15 percent. You owe taxes of $450, and you have a net gain of $2,550. You picked up a $600 arbitrage of the tax system (by receiving a $1,050 tax savings in March 2009 and paying only $450 in March 2010), and gained the time value of the tax savings for a full year. Note that you did not have to sell the fund in March 2010. If you'd continued to hold it, the tax on any unrealized gain would be deferred until the fund was sold. State taxes, if applicable, should also be considered.

Swapping Back

After the wash sale time period has expired, you will likely want to swap back into the original holding. That can create further tax problems. If there is a further loss, there is no problem, as you simply harvest it. However, if there is a gain, it will be short term and taxed at ordinary income-tax rates. Generally, you much prefer to pay taxes at the long-term capital gains rate. Harvesting the prior losses has mitigated part of the problem. You can use the loss to offset gains. By selling only when a reasonably large loss is being harvested (see below), you can maximize the likelihood the harvest ends up being an overall benefit. If the gain during the thirty-one day period required to avoid the wash sale rule in the replacement investment is smaller than the harvested loss, and the replacement fund is not as tax-efficient an investment, then it is generally best to swap back, even if this uses up some of the harvested losses.

Even if the gain is slightly higher than the harvested loss, you may still want to swap back in thirty-one days. For example, if you have swapped a tax-managed fund with a non-tax-managed one, in December you may face even larger capital gain distributions from the replacement investment. A swap back might be warranted.

On the other hand, if the gain from the replacement property is large (for example, 5 percent greater than the harvested loss), you should hold on to the replacement property until the gain becomes long term or prices drop again and swapping back to the original position can be done at low or even no short-term capital gains. In this case, it is recommended you watch the distribution estimates for the replacement investment to make sure distributions won't be greater than the short-term gain you are trying to avoid. In that instance, you should swap back to the more tax-efficient investment before the distribution.

By waiting until the gain becomes long term, the gain could become substantially larger. You don't want to pay taxes, even at longer-term rates. You want a swap holding that is both a suitable replacement in terms of asset class exposure and tax efficient (if such an alternative exists), so you are comfortable holding for the long term, if necessary.

In short, to reduce risks, we suggest taking only significant losses. You should establish a minimum percentage loss of the invested assets and a minimum absolute dollar. A loss is large enough to consider harvesting when it exceeds a predetermined hurdle. For example, you might set a hurdle of $5,000 for bonds and 2 percent of the value. For equities, hurdles of $5,000 and 5 percent might be set. However, for highly volatile asset classes like emerging markets or commodities (remembering that in most cases commodities should be held in tax-deferred accounts), the hurdles might be $5,000 and 7.5 percent. The better the fit in terms of asset class exposure and greater the tax efficiency of the fund you are swapping into (while avoiding investments "substantially identical" to the original holding), the lower the hurdles.

Using ETFs

Because of their tax efficiency and absence of redemption fees imposed by some mutual funds, exchange-traded funds make good candidates for tax loss harvesting purposes. However, because of their high trading volume, a significant amount of their dividend distributions are not considered qualified dividends, and so are taxed at ordinary income tax rates.

When Does Similar Become Too Similar?

There are several mutual funds and ETFs that make good substitutes for one another. To avoid the wash sale rule, the investor cannot sell and buy two investments considered "substantially identical" in nature; the IRS would likely disallow the deduction. For example, selling one S&P 500 Index fund and using the proceeds to buy another S&P 500 Index Fund is not recommended. Instead, an investor might purchase a Russell 1000 Fund. Its risk and expected return is substantially similar, but not substantially identical, thereby avoiding the wash rule. The sale of a tax managed fund and purchase of a non-tax-managed fund in the same asset class would not constitute a wash sale. Always consult with a qualified tax adviser.

For individual bonds, the replacement bond must be "materially different" from the one sold. Although this term appears in the tax code and numerous IRS rulings, no specific rules define what makes one bond materially different from another. Also note that when swapping individual bonds for loss harvesting purposes, there is no need to reverse the swap after thirty-one days.

What if Capital Gains Taxes Rise in the Coming Years?

An increase in tax rates, including capital gains tax rates, may have a substantial impact on a portfolio, and so should be considered when harvesting losses. For investors who may need to take withdrawals from their taxable accounts in the near future (to buy a house or support children in college), harvesting tax losses will reset the cost basis lower and may hurt more than help. A tax loss harvest may save an investor 15 percent in capital gains taxes (the rate at the time of this writing), but could cause the investor to pay an increased rate (20 percent or 28 percent) in the future on an even lower cost basis. This issue will have less effect on investors who do not expect to need withdrawals from their taxable accounts for many years.

There is one other point to consider: If you (1) have gains; (2) will need the money within a few years; and (3) believe tax rates will rise or your own tax bracket will be higher, you may want to harvest gains now to minimize total taxes.

Avoiding the Wash Sale Rule

The IRS prohibits claiming a loss on the sale of an investment if that same or substantially similar investment was purchased within thirty days before or after the sale date. The investor has a choice: Stay out of the market for thirty days after a tax loss harvesting transaction, or immediately purchase a similar but not substantially identical investment. Since a large percentage of the return over any long period typically comes in short bursts, we recommend immediately reinvesting the proceeds. If you are out of the market, you can miss out on those returns. From 1926 through 2008, 169 out of 996 months (17.0 percent) produced returns to the total market in excess of 5 percent. Twenty-nine months had returns in excess of 10 percent, four in excess of 20 percent, and three in excess of 30 percent. Being out of the market for a month also meant you had a 10.1 percent chance (101 months out of 996) of avoiding a loss of at least 5 percent. So, historically, there has been a 70 percent greater likelihood you would "miss" a large gain instead of a large loss.

Given this evidence, the strategy should be to immediately reinvest the proceeds from any loss harvesting sales in similar funds. If there is another loss after thirty-one days the investor can swap back and receive yet another deduction, and again reset the cost basis. The evidence suggests there is about a one-in-six chance of having a gain in excess of 5 percent within the wash sale window. It is important to choose a substitute fund you would be willing to hold for a full year (in order to obtain long-term capital gains treatment) or longer. Any choice should be low cost and tax efficient.

Other Tax Management Strategies

- Sales should be managed on the individual lot basis. When selling shares, to minimize gains and maximize losses, investors should generally choose the highest cost-basis purchases to sell first. This involves keeping track of the cost basis of each share purchased.
- In general, never intentionally realize significant short-term gains. Don't sell any shares until the holding period is sufficient to qualify for the lower long-term capital-gain rate. If your equity allocation is well above target, you may wish to override this suggestion, weighing the risks of an "excessive" allocation to equities versus the potential tax savings.
- If a fund has been held for more than a year, always check to see what estimated distributions the fund plans to make during the year. Specifically focus on amounts that will be ordinary income, short-term capital gains and long-term capital gains. Most funds make distributions once a year, usually near the end of the year. Some make them more frequently, and sometimes they make special distributions. Check to see whether there are going to be large distributions that will be treated as either ordinary income or short-term gains. If this is true, you might benefit from selling the fund before the record date. By doing so, the increase in the net asset value

will be treated as long-term capital gains, and taxes will be at the lower long-term rate. If the fund making the large payout is selling for less than your tax basis, consider selling the fund prior to the distribution. Otherwise, you will have to pay taxes on the distribution, despite having an unrealized loss on the fund. Also consider the potential distribution from the replacement fund so that you don't exacerbate the problem.

Investors should coordinate any tax-planning activities with their CPA or tax attorney to ensure all activity is beneficial to their overall situation, not just when viewed in isolation.

Final Considerations

Following are some additional considerations to be addressed prior to implementing tax loss harvesting:

- Any associated trading costs should be evaluated to ensure they do not exceed the value of the tax benefit.
- Be careful with reinvested dividends: They could trigger a wash sale if it occurs within thirty days.
- An investor might consider immediately repurchasing the sold security inside the investor's tax-advantaged account. This will not work because the IRS considers this a wash sale.

PART IV

THE INVESTMENT PLAN AND FINANCIAL SECURITY

12

College Savings Plans

There are several different approaches to saving for college. We will analyze the benefits and drawbacks of the major ones.

529 Plans

A 529 plan is a tax-advantaged college savings vehicle that lets you save money for college in an individual investment account. In some, you enroll directly. Others require you to go through a financial professional.

Features

- **Federal tax advantages.** Earnings on contributions to your account are completely tax free if the money is used to pay the beneficiary's qualified education expenses. The earnings portion of any withdrawal not used for college expenses is taxed at the recipient's rate and subject to a 10 percent federal penalty.
- **State tax advantages.** Many states offer income tax incentives for state residents (tax deductions for contributions or a tax exemptions for qualified withdrawals, with earnings also tax deferred or tax free). Some states limit their tax deduction to contributions made only to the in-state 529 plan.
- **High contribution limits.** Most college savings plans have lifetime maximum contribution limits.
- **Unlimited participation.** Anyone can open a 529 college savings plan account, regardless of income level.

- **Flexibility.** Under federal rules, you can change the beneficiary of your account to a qualified family member at any time without penalty. You can roll over the money in your 529 plan account to a different 529 plan once per year without income tax or penalty implications.
- **Wide use of funds.** Money in a 529 college savings plan can be used at any college in the United States or abroad that is accredited by the U.S. Department of Education. Depending on the individual plan, funds can also be used for graduate school.
- **Accelerated gifting.** 529 plans offer an excellent estate planning advantage in the form of accelerated gifting. This can be a favorable way for grandparents to contribute to their grandchildren's college educations. The annual limit on contributions for individuals is $13,000 and $26,000 for joint filers. Individuals are able to make a lump-sum gift to a 529 plan of up to $65,000 ($130,000 for married couples) and avoid federal gift tax, provided a special election is made to treat the gift as having been made in equal installments over a five-year period and no other gifts were made to that beneficiary during the five years.
- **Variety.** Currently, there are over fifty different college savings plans to choose from. Many states offer more than one plan, and you can join any of them.
- **Favorable treatment for federal financial support.** Assets are deemed to be owned by the parents.

Prepaid Tuition Plans

Prepaid tuition plans are distant cousins to college savings plans: Their federal tax treatment is the same, but just about everything else is different. A prepaid tuition plan is a tax-advantaged college savings vehicle that lets you pay tuition expenses to participating colleges at today's prices for use in the future. Prepaid tuition plans can be run either by states or by colleges. For state-run plans, you prepay tuition at one or more state colleges. For college-run plans, you prepay tuition at the participating college.

Features

- **Tuition credits.** As with 529 college savings plans, you fill out an application and name a beneficiary. But instead of choosing an investment portfolio, you purchase an amount of tuition credits or units (which you can do again periodically), subject to plan rules and limits. Typically, the tuition credits or units are guaranteed to be worth a certain amount of tuition in the future, no matter how much college costs may increase between now and then. As such, prepaid tuition plans provide a measure of security over rising college prices.

- **Flexibility.** They are open to people of all income levels and offer the flexibility of changing the beneficiary or rolling over to another 529 plan once per year, as well as the option of accelerated gifting. Federal and state tax advantages given to prepaid tuition plans are the same as for college savings plans.
- **Financial support.** For purposes of eligibility for federal financial support, prepaid tuition plans are deemed to be owned by the parents. However, individual institutions and states can treat them differently.
- **Participating plans.** Your child is generally limited to your own state's prepaid tuition plan, and to the colleges that participate in that plan. If your child attends a different college, prepaid plans differ on how much money you'll get back.
- **Benefit reduction.** Some prepaid plans have been forced to reduce benefits after enrollment due to investment returns that have not kept pace with the plan's offered benefits.

Coverdell Education Savings Accounts

A Coverdell education savings account (Coverdell ESA) is a tax-advantaged education savings vehicle that allows you to save money for college, as well as for elementary and secondary school (K–12) at public, private, or religious schools.

Features

- **Contribution rules.** The beneficiary of the Coverdell ESA must be younger than 18 at the time the contribution is made. You (or someone else) make contributions to the account, subject to the maximum annual limit of $2,000. The total amount contributed for a particular beneficiary in a given year can't exceed $2,000, even if the money comes from different people. Contributions can be made up until April 15 of the year following the tax year for which the contribution is being made.

- **Investing contributions.** You invest your contributions as you wish (stocks, bonds, mutual funds, certificates of deposit). You have sole control over your investments.
- **Favorable treatment for federal financial support.** The assets are deemed to be owned by the parents.
- **Tax treatment.** Contributions to your account grow tax deferred. Money withdrawn to pay college or K–12 expenses (called a qualified withdrawal) is completely tax-free at the federal level, and, typically, at the state level as well. If the money isn't used for college or K–12 expenses (called a nonqualified withdrawal), the earnings portion of the withdrawal will be taxed at the beneficiary's tax rate and subject to a 10 percent federal penalty.
- **Rollovers and termination of account.** Funds in a Coverdell ESA can be rolled over without penalty into another Coverdell ESA for a qualifying family member. Also, any funds remaining in a Coverdell ESA must be distributed to the beneficiary when he or she reaches age thirty, unless the beneficiary is a person with special needs.
- **Income limits.** Your ability to contribute depends on your income. To make a full contribution, single filers must have a modified adjusted gross income (MAGI) of $95,000 or less, and joint filers a MAGI of $190,000 or less. With an annual maximum contribution limit of $2,000, a Coverdell ESA probably can't go it alone in meeting today's college costs.

Custodial Accounts

A custodial account allows your child to hold assets under the watchful eye of a designated custodian—assets she ordinarily wouldn't be allowed to hold in her own name. The assets can be used to pay for college or anything else benefiting your child (summer camp, braces, hockey lessons, or a computer).

Features

- Custodian. You designate a custodian to manage and invest the account's assets. The custodian can be you, a friend, a relative, or a financial institution. The custodian controls the assets.
- Assets. You (or someone else) contribute assets to the account. The type of assets you can contribute depends on whether

your state has enacted the Uniform Gifts to Minors Act (UGMA) or the Uniform Transfers to Minors Act (UTMA). Typically contributed are cash, stocks, bonds, mutual funds, and real property.

- Tax treatment. Every year, earnings, interest, and capital gains generated from assets in the account are taxable income of the child. Assuming your child is in a lower tax bracket than you, you'll reap some tax savings compared to holding the assets in your own name. However, this opportunity is limited because of special, "kiddie tax" rules that apply when a child has unearned income: Dependent children with unearned income (dividends, interest, and capital gains) in excess of $1,900 are taxed at the parent's marginal tax rate. This means full-time college students under the age of twenty-four may be subject to the tax. There is an exception for college students at least nineteen years old, and for eighteen-year-olds who are not yet in college and who can demonstrate that their earned income for the year exceeds one-half of their total support.

A custodial account provides the opportunity for some tax savings. However, the kiddie tax sharply reduces the overall effectiveness of custodial accounts as a tax-advantaged college savings strategy. There are other drawbacks: All gifts to a custodial account are irrevocable, and when your child reaches the age of majority (eighteen or twenty-one), the account terminates and your child gains full control of all the assets in the account. Some children may not be able to handle this responsibility, or they might decide not to spend the money for college.

U.S. Savings Bonds

Series EE and Series I (inflation-protected) bonds are types of savings bonds issued by the federal government offering a special tax benefit for college savers. The bonds can be purchased from most neighborhood banks and savings institutions or directly from the federal government. They are available in face values ranging from $50 to $10,000. You may purchase the bond in electronic form at face value or in paper form at half its face value. If the bond is used to pay qualified education expenses, and you meet income limits (as well as a few other minor requirements), the bond's earnings are exempt from federal income tax. The interest on these bonds is always exempt from state and local tax.

These bonds are backed by the full faith and credit of the federal government. Series I bonds offer the added measure of protection against inflation by paying you both a fixed interest rate for the life of the bond (like a Series EE bond) and a variable interest rate adjusted twice a year for inflation. There is a limit on the amount of bonds you can buy in one year, as well as a minimum waiting period before you can redeem the bonds, with a penalty for early redemption.

Financial Aid Impact

Your college saving decisions impact the financial aid process. Come financial aid time, your family's income and assets are run through a formula at both the federal level and the college/institutional level to determine how much money your family should be expected to contribute to college costs prior to receiving any financial aid. This number is referred to as the expected family contribution (EFC).

In the federal calculation, your child's assets are treated differently than your own. Your child must contribute 20 percent of his or her assets each year and you must contribute 5.6 percent of your assets.

For example, $10,000 in your child's bank account would equal an expected child contribution of $2,000 ($10,000 × .20). That same $10,000 in your bank account would equal an expected $560 contribution from you ($10,000 × .056).

Under the federal rules, an UGMA/UTMA custodial account is classified as a student asset. By contrast, 529 plans and Coverdell ESAs are considered parental assets if the parent is the account owner (so accounts owned by grandparents or other relatives or friends do not count). Distributions (withdrawals) from 529 plans and Coverdell ESAs used to pay the beneficiary's qualified education expenses are not classified as parent or student income on the federal government's aid form. This means some or all of the money is not counted again when withdrawn.

Regarding institutional aid, colleges tend to be stricter than the federal government in assessing a family's assets and ability to pay college costs. Most use a standard financial aid application that considers assets the federal government does not (such as home equity). Typically, though, colleges treat 529 plans, Coverdell accounts, and UGMA/UTMA custodial accounts the same as does the federal government, with the caveat that distributions from 529 plans and Coverdell accounts are often counted as available income.

CHAPTER 13

Insurance

As we have discussed, having a well-designed investment plan is only a necessary condition for investment success. The sufficient condition is integrating it into a well-designed estate, tax, and risk management plan. There are noninvestment risks to consider: mortality, disability, the need for long-term care, and even longevity risk (living longer than expected). If these risks are not integrated into the overall financial plan, even the best investment plan can fail. Consider this example.

John is a thirty-two-year-old investment adviser. He is married and has two young children. He has just finished paying off his college debts, and his income is now sufficient to begin saving (and investing) significant amounts. He has a well-designed investment plan. Unfortunately, John dies in an auto accident. While he had a good investment plan, he did not live long enough to execute it. If he did not have enough life insurance his family will not have sufficient resources to provide for the standard of living John desired.

Analyzing the need for life, health, long-term care, disability, and umbrella coverage is a critical part of the financial-planning process. All types of "personal lines" insurance should be considered, so reviewing all existing policies with a personal lines specialist (home, auto, liability, boats, and art) can add significant value.

Risk Management

There are three main points underlying the philosophy of managing insurance risk:

- Insurance should be provided by the highest-rated insurance companies.
- Life insurance contracts should not take investment risk.
- Life insurance contracts should have contractually guaranteed death benefits.

Company Quality

Choosing only from among the highest-rated insurers is critical:

- Credit risk is positively correlated with the length of the horizon: the longer the term, the greater the credit risk. With many forms of insurance, the horizon can be decades long.
- Unlike equity investing, in most cases it is more difficult and costly to diversify the credit risk of insurers. The lower the credit rating, the more important the diversification.

There are several ways to check an insurer's credit worthiness. Joseph Belth, PhD, professor emeritus from Indiana University, has established widely accepted academic standards for evaluating insurance companies. Every September, Belth publishes a ratings issue of his *Insurance Forum* newsletter. Moody's, Standard & Poor's, Fitch, and A.M. Best also publish ratings. Only buy insurance from companies with the highest rating.

Investment Risk

Taking investment risk inside an insurance contract should be avoided because doing so can jeopardize the death benefit. In fact, life insurance should not be viewed as part of the investment strategy, but rather as a tool to achieve an objective. Other reasons to avoid investment risk inside of an insurance contract:

- Investment options are often limited to actively managed options with high internal expense charges and lack proper diversification.

- Mortality and administrative charges are an additional layer of expense reducing returns. If the investment is made outside the insurance contract, those expenses are avoided.

Guaranteed Death Benefits

While many insurance contracts are considered "permanent"—their coverage is not limited to a number of years—that does not mean the contract is guaranteed to provide the death benefit in the future. Only three types guarantee death benefits: term life (for the term of the contract), whole life, and guaranteed death benefit universal life. Of course, the guarantees only apply if the required payments are made. Note that whole life and guaranteed universal life can have the death benefit guaranteed for different periods of time. For example, a whole life policy might mature at age one hundred or age 120, depending on the issuing company. Guaranteed universal life can be arranged with premiums to guarantee a death benefit for a specific number of years or up to age 120, also dependent on the issuing company.

Term Life

Term life insurance provides a death benefit as long as premiums are paid for a period of time. For level premium term, the premiums are level for a set number of years. After that point, they can dramatically increase.

Whole Life

Whole life insurance provides a guaranteed death benefit and does not take investment risk. As long as premiums are paid, the policy death benefit will be guaranteed.

Guaranteed Death Benefit Universal Life

Guaranteed death benefit universal life is essentially term insurance until you die. The typical interest rate assumption in universal life contracts is stripped away and provides a guarantee for life (usually age 110 or 120). These contracts provide no cash value access or growth of death benefit over time, but they generally cost less than whole life.

Universal and Variable Life: Not Recommended

Universal life insurance is the equivalent of a term insurance policy with a fixed annuity rider. As the insured ages, the insurance expense ramps up. If the crediting interest rate and premiums combined are insufficient to cover these costs, premiums will rise. In addition, charges assessed to the policy can be increased to maximum levels at the company's discretion, further diminishing the contract's long-term viability.

Variable universal life is equivalent to a term insurance policy with a variable annuity rider. It has the same issues as universal life, the difference being that it is a mutual fund subaccount—not an interest rate—with returns determining the policy's cash value. Rapidly rising expenses and poor investment options can cause these policies to lapse without large premium payments made later in life, when most investors can least afford to pay them.

Variable Whole Life—Not Recommended

With variable whole life, the majority of premiums pay for a guaranteed base death benefit. The rest is allocated to mutual fund subaccounts that grow the cash value and death benefit. Because the excess premium is being invested inside an insurance contract when the insured could get more cost-effective market exposure elsewhere, this type of coverage is not recommended.

Payout Annuities

We buy insurance to protect our homes, cars, and lives, transferring some or all of risks we prefer not to bear ourselves. So, buying insurance is really about diversifying risks we find unacceptable to bear because the costs of not being insured are too great. The same logic applies to the purchase of payout annuities, the payments of which can be in either nominal or inflation-adjusted dollars.

At its most basic level, deciding to purchase an immediate annuity is a decision to insure against longevity risk: the risk of outliving one's financial assets. As the "cost" of outliving one's financial assets is extremely high, for individuals running that risk purchasing payout annuities makes sense. You should carefully consider their benefits.

Longevity Risk

Consider the following: A healthy male (female) at age sixty-five has a 50 percent chance of living beyond the age of eighty-five (eighty-eight) and a 25 percent chance of living beyond the age of ninety-two (ninety-four). For a healthy couple, both sixty-five, there is a 50 percent chance one will live beyond the age of ninety-two and a 25 percent chance one will live beyond the age of ninety-seven.

When Annuities Can Be the Right Choice

Typically we find that the most appropriate candidates for payout annuities are those whose portfolios are borderline for supporting their desired lifestyle throughout retirement. We recommend using a Monte Carlo simulation to analyze the benefits of a payout annuity.

Application: The following example illustrates why fixed annuities can be an appropriate investment in the right circumstance. John and Jane Smith are both sixty-five. They realize their portfolio is of relatively modest size. When combined with their retirement income from Social Security, it is just enough to provide for a comfortable retirement. They would like to be able to spend a bit more in retirement and have more "margin for error." But they do not want to take any action increasing their chance of running out of money during retirement.

They are concerned they might live longer than expected and have insufficient assets to fund their desired spending in their later years. Further, they are worried that if they do live beyond their life expectancies, their two sons might have to help them financially. Their worst fear is becoming financially dependent on their children.

While they would like to leave a modest estate to their sons, this goal is of minor importance relative to that of not becoming dependent on their children. They are secure in the knowledge their children have both been successful and have their own financial affairs in good order.

Purchasing a payout annuity could provide the Smiths the peace of mind they seek. The higher "return" from mortality credits combined with the guaranteed payments for life could help them achieve their desired standard of living and decreases the risk of outliving their assets and becoming a financial burden on their children.

The concept of a mortality credit is illustrated by the following example. On January 1, we have fifty eighty-five-year-old males who each agree to contribute $100 to a pool of investments earning 5 percent. They further agree to split the total pool equally among those who are still alive at the end of the year. Also, suppose that we (but not them) know for certain that five of the fifty will pass away by the end of the year. This means the total pool of $5,250 ($5,000 principal plus $250 interest) will be split among just forty-five people. Each will receive $116.67, or a return on investment of 16.67 percent. If each person had invested independent of the pool, the total amount of money earned would have been $105 or a return on investment of 5 percent. The difference in returns is the mortality credit.

For the Smiths, the benefits provided by the mortality credits and the guaranteed payments for life outweigh the loss of liquidity and the potential reduction in the value of the estate should they die before their life expectancies.

When to Purchase a Fixed Annuity

In general, the research indicates it is preferable to delay annuitization until the mid 70s or early 80s. One study concluded that a sixty-five-year-old female has an 85 percent chance of being able to beat the rate of return from a life annuity until age eighty. For males, the figure was 80 percent. Thus, unless investors are highly risk averse, they should probably not buy an immediate fixed annuity until they reach their mid to late seventies.

We offer two caveats: There are risks in delaying the purchase of an immediate annuity. First, if life expectancy increases, the cost of the annuity will increase. A 2006 study calculated that a 1 percent annual improvement in mortality is associated with roughly a 5 percent increase in the price of an annuity, or a 5 percent reduction in monthly payouts.[1] Second, if interest rates fall, annuitizing at a later date will lead to lower monthly payouts.

Why Aren't More Payout Annuities Purchased?

While payout annuities increase the odds of investors not depleting their financial assets, very few are purchased and very few deferred annuities are annuitized. The main reason for this anomaly is what we might call "buyers' regret": If they die before their expected lifespan, the assets used to purchase the annuity will be lost to the estate. Of course, if they live longer than expected, assets are preserved. By delaying annuitization until the age of eighty-five, a sixty-five-year-old investor can dramatically reduce the amount of dollars needed to purchase a fixed-income stream, retaining assets for the estate.

Recommended Reading

If you wish to learn more about the benefits of payout annuities, read Chapter 5 of *The Only Guide to Alternative Investments You'll Ever Need.*

Long-Term Care Insurance (LTCI)

It is estimated that at least 60 percent of people over age sixty-five will require some long-term care services. Medicare and private health insurance programs do not pay for the majority of long-term care services most people need, such as help with dressing or using the bathroom.

To get the care you might need, planning is essential. Yet long-term care is often overlooked as a crucial planning tool. According to an April 2007 article in *Financial Planning,* only seven million of the nation's 76 million baby boomers actually have a policy that will cover the costs of long-term care.

Why People Fail to Plan

There are many reasons why people fail to plan for long-term care: the natural tendency to avoid thinking about becoming dependent on others for your care, misinformation about the risks of needing care, and lack of knowledge about the cost of care and payment options. In addition, most people just don't like to think about these types of issues.

Understanding the Product

LTCI can provide for personal and custodial care for an extended period of time. Coverage is triggered by needing help with or losing at least two activities of daily living (ADLs). There are six categories: bathing, dressing, eating, transferring, toileting, and continence.

The "loss of ADLs" could be the need for substantial hands on, standby, or supervisory assistance. Any cognitive impairment, such as Alzheimer's or dementia, are automatically covered whether or not the two-ADL trigger is met.

A common misperception of long-term care is that it is only for nursing home care. While care may be received at a nursing home, it can also be received at an assisted living facility, adult day care with respite services, or for home-based care. Care can be defined in two ways:

- Care for custodial (personal) needs. Care provided to assist with ADLs or to meet personal needs (assistance with bathing, dressing, eating, or getting in or out of bed).
- Care for skilled needs. Care provided by a licensed health care professional such as an RN, LPN, physical therapist, or speech therapist. A physician must order this care.

Long-term care is a tool that can help preserve and protect financial assets. It provides flexibility in choosing the type of care and where care is received. It can help ensure high-quality care and provide financial and emotional support for the family. There are six issues to consider when purchasing long-term care coverage:

1. How much coverage is right for you?
   - What is the cost of care in your area?
   - What daily benefit amount (DBA) would you need and want? (These may be two different answers.)
2. Where would you like to receive care?
   - Nursing home
   - Home-based health care
3. How would you like to receive your benefits?
   - Reimbursement: Reimbursement for actual expenses accrued on a monthly basis.
   - Indemnity: Full DBA payments when receiving licensed care whether or not maximum DBA is being used, that is, full payment of DBA for each day of care no matter how much is spent.
   - Cash: This does not require licensed care. It is the most expensive option, up to 20 percent additional cost.

4. How long do you want to receive benefits?
   - Typical benefit periods are two, three, five, seven, and ten years (this is carrier specific).
   - Lifetime option is available but seldom used.
   - Benefit period is driven by a pool of money. *Example:* A $150 DBA × 365 days × 5 years = $273,750 total lifetime benefits. Even if five years have elapsed, the benefit remains until the pool of money is depleted.
5. What type of inflation protection would you like?
   - None
   - Simple. Typically 5 percent.
   - Compound. Also typically 5 percent.
6. How long can you wait before benefits are paid?
   - The "elimination period" is the period of time during which you are responsible for paying the cost of your care services.
   - A typical elimination period is ninety to one-hundred days.

The Importance of Long-Term Care: A Monte Carlo Analysis

Using the tool of Monte Carlo analysis, the following case study demonstrates the importance of long-term care.

Mr. and Mrs. Smith are both sixty-five years old. They have financial assets of $6 million. A Monte Carlo analysis reveals that their portfolio has a high likelihood of providing sufficient assets to maintain their desired lifestyle if neither ever has a need for long-term care. If one or both need long-term care for an extended period, the portfolio has a significant likelihood of being strained or even depleted. The Monte Carlo analysis also reveals that the costs of a LTCI policy will not significantly reduce the odds of success.

If no insurance is needed, the costs of purchasing a long-term care policy increases the odds of running out of money by just 3 percent (94 to 91 percent). If long-term care is needed, and no insurance purchased, the odds of running out of money increase by 20 percent: the odds of success falling from 94 to 74 percent (see Table 13.1). That is almost seven times the 3 percent increase in likelihood of failure caused by the purchase of insurance.

For some affluent investors, the analysis may show they can self-insure and still have sufficiently low odds of failure, that is, outliving

Table 13.1   The Impact of Adding Long-Term Care Insurance

Long-Term Care Scenarios*	Odds the Portfolio Will Have Sufficient Assets (%)
No long-term care insurance, no need for care	94
Have long-term care insurance, no need for care	91
Have long-term care insurance coverage for 20 years, need care for 5 years (age 85–90)	83
No long-term care insurance, need care from age 85–90	74

sufficient financial assets. Let's take an investor with substantial bequeath objectives and analyze her likelihood of having at least $1 million, $3 million, or $5 million at death (see Table 13.2).

Table 13.2   The Impact of Adding Long-Term Care Insurance

Long-Term Care Scenarios*	Odds Ending Portfolio Will Have at Least $1mm, $3mm, and $5mm
No long-term care insurance, no need for care	94%, 68%, 48%
Have long-term care insurance, no need for care	91%, 63%, 45%
Have long-term care insurance coverage for 20 years, need care for 5 years (age 85–90)	83%, 55%, 38%
No long-term care insurance, need care from age 85–90	74%, 49%, 32%

*The following assumptions are used in the above analysis:
LTCI Policy Coverages

- Five years of benefit
- $200/day in benefit
- Shared care (ten total years if needed)
- Indemnity (no receipts needed)
- Compound inflation
- Premium: $10,500 per year total
- Elimination period: 100 days

Care assumptions without LTC:

- $750/day for five years.
- Both people need some care and are most likely at home for the five-year period age 85–90. This adds $273,750 per year in living needs.

Care assumptions with LTC insurance:

- $750/day for five years Subtract $350 (assumed the coverage was needed, leaving the self insuring amount at $400). This adds $127,750 per year in living needs.

The addition or absence of long-term care significantly impacts the odds of success.

We see that while the odds of leaving a large estate decrease somewhat if long-term care insurance is purchased and no care is needed, the odds of success fall by a greater amount if long-term care insurance is not purchased and care is needed. Thus, both risk-averse individuals and those with large bequeath objectives should prefer to purchase such insurance.

Life Settlements

Traditional life settlements offer policyholders the opportunity to access additional cash by unloading policies they no longer need or can afford. Recently, the industry has seen the emergence of speculator-initiated life insurance policies, or "spin-life policies" that promote the purchase of life insurance only to sell it to an investor a few years later for a single payment. While traditional life settlements can be useful tools for financial and estate planners, a spin-life strategy is not recommended as the benefits do not outweigh the costs and inherent risks.

Background

Purchasers of life settlements are generally large institutions like banks or hedge funds. The ideal policyholder is an older individual (sixty-five or older) who can no longer afford the premiums or no longer needs the death benefits from a life insurance policy. Life-settlement investors pool the purchased policies, dividing them into life-settlement-backed securities typically sold to hedge funds, pension funds, and other institutional investors.

Life-settlement brokers are also in the market. While some help investors sell their existing policies to other investors, others are taking a more aggressive approach. Some brokers seek out older high-net-worth individuals with life insurance capacity, lend them money to pay for premiums on high-value life insurance policies, and prearrange to purchase the policy a few years later for a one-time cash payout (less the amount loaned for the premiums). These speculator-initiated spin-life contracts are also known as stranger-owned life insurance (STOLI) policies.

Benefits

Selling policies to fund medical care and living expenses is referred to as traditional life settlements. With anticipated changes to estate-tax laws, traditional life-settlements can provide investors with an additional estate and financial planning tool. For example, a life settlement could be used to remove the value of an individually held life insurance policy from an estate's assets. A charitable organization receiving a donated life insurance policy can use a life settlement to receive an immediate cash benefit with no further premium obligations. The donor would receive a tax deduction from the donation and an additional amount in excess of the surrender value from the life-settlement transaction.

Risks

Life-settlement payouts are often about a third of policy value and much greater than the surrender value or cash value of the contract.[2] There is no official guidance from the IRS regarding the tax treatment of life settlements. The IRS could consider all proceeds above the cost basis as ordinary income—not the industry's customary tax treatment.[3] There are trade-offs, as "the tax consequences to the seller of receiving a cash payment during the insured's lifetime are not as favorable (or certain) as that of receiving the policy's death benefit."[4] You should consult a tax expert prior to arranging for a life-settlement payout.

Opaqueness of the Bidding Process

One big obstacle to completing a traditional life-settlement transaction is finding an investor. Individuals should always obtain more than one bid for their policies and request full transparency during the bidding process. There is evidence that in some cases, brokers negotiated settlements and did not pass along the full bid amounts to the clients.[5] According to a study conducted by Deloitte, seniors completing a life-settlement transaction received just 20 cents on the dollar instead of the 64 cents on the dollar Deloitte calculated to be the intrinsic value of the policy.[6]

Where policies contain personal data and medical history, sellers should verify that investors are well-established institutions that will transfer such information anonymously. If personal information is known, one can argue the insured risks a moral hazard.

Industry regulations have not been firmly established in this new industry, and there have been several well-publicized life-settlement investigations and lawsuits. As more regulations are adopted, there may be fewer investors to offer liquidity from insurance policies, and the ability to sell policies and transfer ownership may become more difficult.

Spin-life policies are also subject to additional risks and costs that traditional life settlements do not face. There is credit risk with the investors, since the insured must both:

- Rely on funds from the investors to pay for the premiums.
- Ensure the investors will have enough capital to purchase the policy.

Carefully review contracts with an insurance expert. Some may include clauses where, if an investor cannot be found, you are not released from the debt or interest on the debt.

Market Changes

Some states are increasing the number of contestable years for life insurance. Some thirty states are currently weighing two- or five-year waiting periods before policyholders can sell their policies. In an effort to target STOLIs directly, others prohibit the sale of a life insurance policy within five years of purchase if the insured borrowed money to pay for the premiums.[7] Finally, a few states are contesting the legality of life settlements. To purchase insurance, one must have an insurable interest (usually in their own lives), but there are currently no laws prohibiting life settlements. Insurance lobbyists are hard at work to make those changes. This could allow insurance companies to cancel or void spin-life policies, leaving the policyholder without a policy to sell and a large amount of debt from loans on the insurance premiums.

Conclusion

Increases in regulations and in life insurance premiums to cover falling lapse ratios (number of lapsed policies to total number of policies in force at the beginning of the year) lead to a more restrictive life-settlements market and one with reduced individual profit. The higher premiums also make it more expensive for individuals who truly need life insurance to purchase new policies. With the legal and tax treatment of STOLI policies so uncertain, and given such lack of transparency in the arrangements, these transactions cannot be recommended. However, traditional life settlements continue to be useful financial and estate planning tools. For individuals who have unnecessary policies and do not need immediate access to a lump sum of cash, there are other options. Some possible alternatives include using a 1035 exchange to convert from an insurance asset to:

- An investment asset (such as a low-cost deferred variable annuity).
- An immediate annuity for income.
- A new life insurance policy.

CHAPTER 14

IRAs and Retirement/Profit Sharing Plans

This chapter focuses on retirement accounts. We begin with the decision on whether to invest in a Roth IRA or a traditional IRA.

Roth versus Traditional IRA

Individual retirement accounts (IRAs) are tax-advantaged investments. The two different types of IRAs—traditional and Roth—have some similarities and some differences. The differences have implications for the development of an investment policy statement, the asset allocation decision, and the choice of the preferred vehicle.

Contributions to a Roth IRA are made on an *after-tax* basis and distributions are not subject to income tax. The traditional IRA is the mirror opposite. It allows contributions to be made on a *pre-tax* basis (on the tax return the adjusted gross income is reduced by the amount of the contribution), but all withdrawals are subject to taxation.

An example will illustrate both the differences and similarities of the two accounts. Consider two investors, John and Mary. Both are in the 25 percent tax bracket. Both expect to be in that same 25 percent bracket when they retire. They also have the same income and spending needs. They both invest on the same day in the same mutual fund. Each has just received a $1,000 bonus. We'll start with John.

John decides he will invest his bonus in a Roth IRA. Having to set aside 25 percent of his bonus to pay federal income taxes, John makes a $750 contribution to his Roth IRA, investing that amount in a mutual fund that invests in equities. John's investments increase in value by 33⅓ percent. He now has $1,000. Assuming no penalty for early withdrawal, John could withdraw $1,000 with no taxes owed. Now let's consider Mary.

Mary decides to use her bonus to contribute $1,000 to her traditional IRA. She can invest $250 more than John because she doesn't have to pay the *current* income tax on the $1,000 invested. Mary invests her $1,000 in the same mutual fund, earning the same 33⅓ percent return. She ends up with $1,333. When she withdraws the funds from her traditional IRA (still assuming no early-withdrawal penalty) she will pay a tax of 25 percent ($333). Like John, she ends up with exactly the same $1,000. That tax of $333 is equal to the original tax that was deferred ($250) plus $83—the 33⅓ percent gain on the $250. Mary was investing funds on behalf of the government, actually owning only 75 percent of her IRA. The government owned the other 25 percent. This example demonstrates five important facts.

Five Key Facts

One

A traditional IRA is identical to a Roth IRA if the tax rate at the time of contribution is the same as the tax rate on withdrawal. Our Mary/John example proves this: Both portfolios generated $1,000 net.

Two

If the same investment in either a Roth or traditional IRA results in the same ending dollars after withdrawal, there is no tax on either. Many people have a hard time understanding this. The right way to think about it is that Mary never owned 100 percent of her $1,000 investment. She owned 75 percent of it; the government owned the other 25 percent. The government let Mary invest its share of the money until she withdrew her share. At that point the government claimed its 25 percent. Mary is in the identical situation as John. Just as there was no tax on John's earnings, there really was no tax on Mary's share of the earnings.

You may often have heard advice that you should not hold equities in a traditional IRA because doing so converts what would otherwise be capital gains into ordinary income. This is incorrect: As the example shows, there is no tax on the gain.

Three

Taxes need to be integrated into investment policy. That Mary only actually owned 75 percent of her $1,000 investment has implications for investment policy and the asset allocation decision. Assume Mary and John each started with $1,000 of equity holdings in taxable accounts. John invests another $750 in his Roth, and Mary invests another $1,000 in her traditional IRA. This time they both put the money into bond funds. What are their respective asset allocations? The conventional analysis would be as follows:

- John has $1,000 in stocks and $750 in bonds. His asset allocation is thus 57 percent stocks and 43 percent bonds.
- Mary's allocation of $1,000 in stocks and $1,000 in bonds is 50/50.

But since the Roth and the traditional IRA are the same, Mary's allocation must actually be the same as John's, not 50/50. Her allocation is the same $1,000 in stocks and $1,000 × [1 minus the 25 percent tax rate], or $750, in bonds. This is the same 57/43 allocation. If Mary wanted to have an allocation of 50/50 her holdings should have been $875 of stocks and $125 of bonds in the taxable account and $1,000 of bonds in the traditional IRA.

The tax code impacts the asset allocation of taxable accounts as well as IRAs. For example, if John had a taxable account that owned an equity mutual fund with a cost basis of $1,000 and a present value of $11,000 (assuming a long-term federal and state capital gains tax of 20 percent and no step-up in basis expected), for the purposes of determining John's asset allocation we would conclude he owned just $9,000 of equities, not $11,000. The government "owns" 2,000 of the 11,000—20 percent of the $10,000 unrealized gain.

We now turn to the issue of what drives the decision of which IRA to purchase.

Four

The decision of making a contribution to a traditional or Roth IRA should be based on whether the tax rate on withdrawal is expected be higher or lower than at the time of contribution. If lower, the preferred choice should be the traditional IRA: the government will own a lower percentage of the investment dollars. Here is an example.

John's tax rate is 25 percent on contribution. He expects it to be just 15 percent on withdrawal. In the original example, John invested $750 in the Roth IRA; given the 331/3 percent return he would be able to withdraw $1,000. If instead he made the contribution to a traditional IRA, he could contribute $1,000, deferring the 25 percent income tax otherwise due. The $1,000 grows to $1,333. With John's income-tax rate just 15 percent at withdrawal, he can withdraw $1,133 ($1,333 × [1 minus 15 percent]). In terms of asset allocation, John owned 85 percent of the account, not 100 percent.

If the tax rate at withdrawal is expected to be *higher* than at contribution, the preferred choice should be the Roth: You pay the government its share when the tax rate is lower. Using John again as an example, assume he is in the 25 percent bracket at contribution but expects to be in the 33 percent bracket on withdrawal. If he invests in the Roth he can invest $750, and he will be able to withdraw $1,000. If he invests in a traditional IRA he can invest $1,000 and withdraw $1,333 before taxes. However, after taxes the net amount is just $893 ($1,333 × [1 minus the 33 percent tax rate]). Thus, when the tax rate is expected to be higher at withdrawal than at contribution the Roth is generally the preferred choice. But there is another consideration.

Maximizing the Benefits of the Tax Code.   The maximum contributions to traditional and Roth IRAs are the same. For 2010, the maximum for those under age fifty was $5,000 and for those over 50 $6,000 (allowing for what is called a "catch up"). Assume Mary and John are both forty, each can contribute the $5,000 maximum and both have sufficient cash flow to make the contribution. Let's look at the implications of John's $5,000 investment in a Roth IRA versus Mary's $5,000 contribution to a traditional IRA.

Mary's $5,000 contribution allows her to save $1,250 of current income taxes. She has $1,250 to invest in a taxable account along with the $5,000 in her traditional IRA, for a total of $6,250. She does not own the full $5,000 of her traditional IRA, only $3,750 ($5,000 × [1 minus the tax rate of 25 percent]). The government owns the remaining $1,250. On her holdings, $3,750 will not be subject to any tax, and $1,250 (in the taxable account) will be subject to taxes on any gains. Her total holdings are $5,000, just like John. However, all of John's $5,000 is in a tax-free (Roth) account. If the tax rates at contribution and withdrawal are expected to be the same, the Roth account is the preferred choice for those that can make the maximum contribution. Doing so allows them to hold more funds in a tax-free environment.

The benefit of the lower tax rate on withdrawal has to be weighed against the benefit of being able to invest more dollars in the tax-free environment. The individual needs to decide which is more valuable: contributing a greater amount to a tax-advantaged account or having the government take a smaller share. Three issues warrant consideration. First, look at the difference in tax rates. The larger the difference, the more it favors the traditional IRA. The second issue is the length of the investment horizon. The longer the period, the more it favors the Roth. Issue three is the level of tax efficiency of your taxable investments. The more tax efficient, the less advantage the Roth provides.

Given that (1) tax rate differences can be large, (2) investors have access to highly tax-efficient investment vehicles (like tax-managed equity funds), and (3) the difference in the additional amount of investment dollars that can be placed in tax-advantaged accounts is relatively small, the traditional IRA would still be the choice if the tax rate is expected to be lower at withdrawal. Given the complexities of the issue, it would still be prudent to seek expert counsel.

The issues related to the ability to maximize contributions also relate to a Roth 401(k). The difference is that the Roth 401(k) is not constrained by the same income limitations or contribution rules constraining a Roth IRA. Employees can decide to contribute funds on a post-tax basis, in addition to or instead of pre-tax deferrals under their traditional 401(k) plans. An employee under the age of fifty could defer [whether to a traditional 401(k), a Roth 401(k), or to both] up to $16,500 for tax year 2010. If over age fifty, they could contribute an additional $5,500, for a total of $22,000. Note that employer contributions (employer match, profit sharing contribution) are always pre-tax; the Roth option is only available for employee contributions.

Since individuals should always try to maximize their contributions to tax-advantaged accounts, the Roth 401(k) is a valuable tool. The same issues apply to 403(b) accounts.

Pay Me Now or Pay Me Later.   As seen from the examples above, it is just a case of when the government's "tax bell tolls." You control the timing. Your choice should be based on when you think the government's percentage ownership is likely to be lower. Since you don't know for certain what future tax rates will be, one strategy is to assume that your future marginal tax rate will be the same as it is today. Another strategy worth considering is diversifying the risk of changing tax rates, splitting contributions between a Roth and a traditional IRA. As your tax rate varies over time you will withdraw more from your Roth when your marginal rate is high and more from the traditional IRA when it is low.

Five

While traditional IRAs require minimum withdrawals (RMDs), Roths do not: The government has already collected its toll (taxes on the income have already been paid). If an individual believes they will not need the RMD to pay for living expenses, choosing the Roth could be better even if the tax rate was expected to be slightly lower at withdrawal. Remember, too, that when estimating future tax rates you should consider the impact of an RMD on the marginal tax rate and on the taxability of Social Security benefits.

There are a few more considerations. If an individual has a traditional IRA but cannot make additional pre-tax contributions because his income exceeds the adjusted gross income (AGI) threshold, he can still make strategic decisions regarding the choice of IRA account. Since the government will take its toll at the time of conversion, you should convert if you expect the tax rate will be lower if you pay the tax now than when you would otherwise begin withdrawals.

One more point: Due to the specific formulas for the calculation of taxes for investors likely to be subject to estate tax, the dollars accumulated in Roth IRAs are, in effect, taxed less heavily than those in a traditional IRA. The formulas are complicated. Those likely to be subject to the estate tax should seek professional estate tax advice from their CPA.

Summary

Integrating tax consequences into investment plans can be complex, especially as tax rates and investment values change. There are two ways to address this problem. The first is to tax adjust your current holdings to account for the government's share. The other approach is to use a Monte Carlo simulation with tax codes built in to determine the odds of success of your investment plan. The simulation will account for the government's share and give you the estimated odds of your plan succeeding in achieving its goal. That goal can range from not outliving your assets to leaving an estate of $X million. The latter approach is recommended for its simplicity. Either will help you make the right decisions.

A final note: We urge caution in using software tools purporting to analyze the benefits of traditional IRA and Roth IRAs. The several we have looked at contain errors, missing some of the key points raised in this chapter.

What to Do When Retirement Plan Choices Are Poor

The historical record provided by academic studies is clear: The prudent investment strategy is investing in low-cost mutual funds that are passively managed: index funds, ETFs, and passive asset class funds. Because of the expenses of providing and maintaining a plan, a conflict of interest can arise between what is best for the employer (least cost) and best for the employee (access to the best investment vehicles). This conflict is very often decided in favor of the employer.

The employer can save a lot of money by not having to pay for administration of the employee benefit. Management gets very interested when a fund family providing high cost, actively managed funds proposes to the employer that they will pick up all of the plan's administrative expenses if the employer makes their fund family the exclusive (or at least dominant) provider of investment alternatives. Because high-cost, active management is a loser's game, it is the employees who lose, accumulating fewer dollars in their retirement accounts.

It would be far better for both employers and employees to choose a plan with low-cost, passive investment vehicles. If the employer could not afford the administrative costs of such a plan, the costs could be unbundled and appropriately passed on to each employee. Employees may be concerned they would be charged for a service that in the past was "free." But through education they will learn they have been paying for administration services all along, just not being billed separately for them. The cost showed up in lower returns earned due to the higher internal expenses of the mutual funds in which they were investing. In the long term, charging employees directly for administration costs is significantly less expensive than paying both the expenses of high-cost mutual fund companies and the extra, and nonproductive, trading costs of active management.

If an employee does not have access to low-cost, passive investment choices the option becomes a choice between the "lesser among evils."

For three reasons, the best choice is to first use the retirement plan for fixed income assets. It is preferable from a tax-efficiency standpoint to hold the equities in taxable accounts and fixed-income assets in tax-advantaged accounts. Index or other passively managed funds should be used, but they are often not available. A second reason: Expense ratios and trading costs of actively managed fixed-income funds are generally lower than for actively managed equity funds. By choosing fixed-income funds, you can reduce total expenses and the drag on returns. Third, the dispersion of returns across bond funds is usually much lower than for stock funds. Actively managed stock funds are more likely to underperform by large amounts than even poor (or lucky) bond funds.

If the investor needs to hold equities in the tax-advantaged account the first choice should be to choose index or other passively managed funds. The preference should be for domestic funds, since the foreign tax credit is lost in tax-advantaged accounts. If passively managed funds are not available, style drift must be considered. Since controlling the risk of a portfolio is of paramount importance, investors should look for funds that "stick to their knitting." Investors should also look for funds having the lowest total expenses (operating expense ratios, other fees, and the lowest turnover): Expenses incurred in selecting securities and/or timing the market are highly likely to prove counterproductive. The bottom line is that investors should look for funds most closely resembling low-cost, passive funds. One example is Vanguard's Windsor Fund, a good choice for gaining exposure to the asset class of U.S. large value. It is low cost, low turnover and has shown no tendency to style drift.

It is important to build a portfolio that is globally diversified by asset class, thereby avoiding placing all your eggs in one asset class basket (U.S. large growth). However, if your only choices are active funds and one index fund (many plans include at least an S&P 500 Index or Total Stock Market fund), invest in the index fund and diversify your equity holdings outside the plan. If the costs of the active choices allowing you to diversify are high, forgo the diversification benefits in favor of the sure savings from lower expenses.

One more point to consider: If the only two index funds in the plan are an S&P 500 Index fund and a total stock market fund with similar expenses, choose the latter. It is more diversified.

IRA Conversions

Limitations

Roth IRAs restrict contribution eligibility. For 2010, investors who were married filing jointly saw their contribution limits phase out once their MAGI exceeded $167,000, and they lost Roth IRA contribution eligibility with a MAGI above $177,000. For those with a filing status of single or head of household, the limits are $105,000 and $120,000, respectively. Qualifying investors can still own a Roth IRA by doing what is called a Roth conversion. This involves converting a traditional IRA into a Roth IRA. Determining if a conversion makes sense is where it gets more complicated.

Who is Eligible for the Roth Conversion?

Unless current tax laws change, income limits for converting traditional IRAs to Roth IRAs will no longer apply. In addition, those who convert in 2010 can stretch the tax liability over two years, with half the conversion amount included in taxable income in 2011 and the other half in 2012. Conversions occurring after 2010 will require the entire conversion amount to be included as income during the year of the conversion.

When considering a conversion, keep the following factors in mind:

- Are sufficient funds available to pay the tax on the amount to be converted? (Remember, you are paying it at ordinary income tax rates.) The greatest potential for growth occurs when funds from taxable accounts are used to pay the taxes.
- An IRA inherited from a person other than a spouse cannot be converted to a Roth IRA.
- Assets must not be withdrawn from the Roth IRA within five years of the conversion. If you do, you will have to pay the 10 percent early distribution penalty, even if you are older than 59½. The five-year withdrawal limitation for IRA conversions begins January 1 of the calendar year the conversion takes place. So, if you convert to a Roth IRA in December 2010, the effective start date for the five years is January 1, 2010. That means you have only four years remaining until the withdrawal penalties disappear.

However, the conversion income could push you into a higher tax bracket, increasing your total tax liability and possibly disqualifying you from other tax benefits such as the dependent child care and college tuition tax credits. It may also push Social Security benefits into taxable income.

Who Should Consider a Roth Conversion?

A Roth conversion may make sense if you answer "yes" to any of the following questions:

- Do you have enough money outside your IRA to meet your needs? Unlike traditional IRAs, Roth IRAs do not have required minimum distributions at 70½. If you want to pass this account untouched to your heirs, conversions make sense.
- Do you need to generate income to take advantage of tax credits or deductions? If you have charitable deductions, carry-forwards, or other tax-favored items, but not much income one year, conversions may make sense. Not only do you get the benefits of conversion, but by forcibly increasing your income (money moved counts as income), you can take advantage of all your qualified deductions and credits.

A conversion can also be helpful for investors with high medical expenses; additional taxable income helps take advantage of the full deduction.

- Do you believe your tax bracket is lower now than it will be in retirement? Conversions may be good for young investors with low income. The tax on the conversion should be low, and it is possible that when the money is withdrawn, a higher tax will later apply on taxable distributions. This would be especially true if the investors have high equity allocations in their Traditional IRA. Equities have high expected returns. The account could grow to sufficiently large levels, making the required minimum distributions large enough to cause their marginal tax rate to be at a high level. The longer the investment horizon, the more important this issue becomes.
- Do you have enough money outside the IRA to pay the taxes on the conversion? Investors converting their IRAs should pay conversion taxes from taxable dollars. Doing so allows for greater growth potential.

Who Should Not Consider a Roth Conversion?

If you answer "yes" to any of the following questions, a Roth conversion may not make sense:

- **Do you believe you are in a higher tax bracket now than you will be in retirement?** The taxes paid to convert now may exceed the taxes paid later at the lower rate on IRA distributions, negating the benefits.
- **Are you interested in leaving your IRA to a charity?** There are no advantages to rolling it into a Roth and paying taxes on it now, since it will be a tax-free event for the charity when received.

Partial Conversions

A partial conversion may make more sense in the following scenarios:

- If you do not have money to comfortably pay the taxes, partial conversions over a set time period would soften the tax impact. As long as you meet the income and filing requirements you can continue to convert a portion every year.

- When you convert money from traditional IRAs to Roth IRAs, it counts as income. If the amount of the conversion would increase taxable income enough to move you into a higher tax bracket, partial conversions may be more sensible. This can be difficult to estimate, so it is important to get your CPA involved.

What if the Conversion Was a Mistake? (Recharacterizations)

What happens if you discover the Roth conversion cannot be made because your AGI unexpectedly (not unhappily) climbed over the allowable limit? Or suppose it would be in your best interest to reverse the conversion (perhaps because of a drop in the value of your investments), converting again at some future date and paying less tax? In either case you can "recharacterize" that conversion (and any earnings thereon) back to a traditional IRA. If you do so in a timely manner, you will not incur any taxes or penalties.

Recharacterizations must take place by the due date of your tax return, including extensions. You must move the Roth IRA funds (and applicable earnings) back to their traditional IRA prior to October 15 of the year following the conversion. If you wait until after the October 15 deadline, you will be required to close the account and pay taxes and penalties on any early distributions.

If you convert traditional IRAs to Roth IRAs and then recharacterize them back to traditional IRAs, you may not reconvert that amount back to Roth IRAs before the later of:

- The first of the following year from when the amounts were originally converted to the Roth IRAs; or
- The end of the 30-day period following the day on which the Roth IRAs were recharacterized back to traditional IRAs.

Any reconversion made before the later of these two dates would be deemed to have "failed."

The Pension Protection Act of 2006

Previously, Roth conversions could only be done from IRAs. There were no rules permitting the same type of conversion from employees' qualified retirement plans. However, effective for tax years after December 31, 2007, the Pension Protection Act of 2006 allows taxpayers to convert all or a portion of their eligible retirement plans to Roth IRAs.

The rules that apply to Roth IRA conversions from traditional IRAs will also apply to conversions from eligible retirement plans. Thus, married taxpayers filing separately will not qualify.

Conversions from Non-Deductible IRAs

If you have only contributed to nondeductible IRAs and wish to convert, part of the conversion will be tax-free. Taxes are calculated only on the earnings from nondeductible contributions, not the nondeductible contributions themselves. However, if you own both deductible and nondeductible IRAs, the taxable portion of the IRA (or portion of the IRA you will convert) will be determined based on the proportion of taxable money in all the traditional and simple IRAs combined. If you have untaxed amounts in other IRAs, you may end up owing more in taxes on this conversion than expected. The IRS does not allow you to designate that your conversions are only from the nondeductible contributions.

Summary

The decision to convert traditional IRAs into Roth IRAs is not easy to make. You will have to make some assumptions regarding both your future tax situation and cash flow needs. It is important to think these things through and consult a tax expert.

CHAPTER 15

Social Security

According to the Social Security Administration (SSA), Social Security benefits represent about 40 percent of income for the elderly. Social Security benefits are guaranteed income that is inflation adjusted, investment risk-free, longevity protected, and comes with a spousal death benefit. Because the benefits are often a significant source of retirement income, it is important to know when to begin taking them to optimize lifetime benefits.

How Benefits are Determined

Benefits are determined based on a claimant's birth year, benefits start date, and lifetime earnings. Once reaching full retirement age (FRA), the worker is eligible for a full retired worker benefit, the primary insurance amount (PIA). Depending on the worker's year of birth, the current FRA ranges from sixty-five to sixty-seven. If a worker claims a benefit prior to reaching the FRA, the PIA can be reduced up to 30 percent. Due to delayed retirement credits, delaying a claim until seventy will result in a benefit of 32 percent over the PIA.

When to Take Benefits

Actuarially, if you live to average life expectancy, taking benefits at any age will provide the same cumulative amount of benefits. Under certain circumstances. you could earn more or less than what is expected. It is in these cases that deciding when to take benefits becomes important.

Factors to Consider

Current health, life expectancy, employment status, and taxes all affect the decision of when to take Social Security benefits. Most retirees are inclined to take them as soon as possible. However, the longer claiming is delayed, the greater the benefits. And larger benefits are beneficial to current retirees when longevity risk (living beyond life expectancy) is an issue.

Taking Benefits Early

The decision to stop working and start receiving Social Security at age sixty-two must factor in whether the individual can afford to live on the reduced benefits versus the higher benefits at age sixty-five. In addition, because an individual cannot qualify for Medicare until age sixty-five, they will be living on less income and have to find medical insurance to cover them the next three years. This insurance is likely to be expensive—if it can even be found.

For individuals in early retirement with no other significant income sources, taking benefits early may be the only option. If health problems force early retirement, consider applying for Social Security disability benefits as well. A qualifying retiree could receive a benefit equal to the PIA through a combination of early Social Security benefit and disability benefit. When reaching their FRA, the benefit will be converted to a full retirement age benefit.

Individuals who believe they have below average life expectancy should consider taking benefits as soon as possible. Some married couples might optimize household benefits by claiming early and collecting more survivor benefits overall.

If you take benefits early to supplement earnings income, $1 of benefits will be deducted for every $2 you earn above the annual limit. For 2010, the limit was $14,160. In the year you reach FRA, $1 of every $3 earned above $37,680 (annual limit for 2010) will be deducted from your benefits. This only includes the earnings in the months prior to reaching FRA. In effect, this creates a temporary 50 percent tax on earnings above the annual limit until you reach FRA, but a permanent reduction in Social Security benefit of up to 25 percent. Once you reach FRA, benefits have no limit on earnings. But this shouldn't completely discourage you from continuing to work while receiving Social Security benefits. The SSA automatically reviews your earnings record, replacing the lowest earnings in your work record with your latest year of earnings, if higher. If you have not already hit the maximum Social Security benefit, these higher earnings could result in a higher benefit.

Delaying Benefits

Delaying Social Security generally optimizes lifetime benefits. This is especially true for married couples due to additional benefits like spousal and survivor benefits. When a primary wage earner has a younger spouse with higher life expectancy, delaying benefits could pay off in the long run. Those who have the financial flexibility to delay until FRA or beyond will receive either the PIA or up to 32 percent over the PIA at age seventy. Delaying potentially offers these benefits:

- Higher guaranteed annuity-like benefit with COLAs (cost-of-living adjustment);
- Higher benefit paid to surviving spouse;
- Higher benefit when maximum Social Security benefits have not yet been reached and a worker continues to work past sixty-two;
- Avoiding the reduction in benefits if collecting Social Security and still earning income before FRA.

Taxes

If total income exceeds a certain level, up to 85 percent of Social Security benefits can be taxed as ordinary income. Social Security income is not taxed in the same way as IRA withdrawals: You can reduce your taxes by choosing higher Social Security income and lower IRA income when developing your strategy for taking retirement income.

To determine taxation of Social Security benefits, calculate your "Combined Income" —Adjusted Gross Income (AGI) + Non-taxable Interest + ½; of Social Security benefits. The Combined Income formula calculates the tax on the *smallest* of:

- 50 percent of the excess over the first threshold (see Table 15.1 below), plus 35 percent of the excess over the second threshold; or
- 85 percent of the benefits; or
- 50 percent of the benefits plus 85 percent of any excess over the second threshold.

Table 15.1   2009 Thresholds for Calculating Taxes on Social Security

	Individual	Married
No tax	Less than $25,000	Less than $32,000
Up to 50 percent taxed	$25,000–$34,000	$32,000–$44,000
Up to 85 percent taxed	$34,001+	$44,001+

Here's an example of a married couple filing jointly:

AGI	$50,000
Tax-free bond interest	2,000
½ of $20,000 in Social Security benefits	10,000
Combined income	$62,000
Excess of income over 1st level ($32,000)	$30,000
Excess of income over 2nd level ($44,000)	$18,000

To calculate the new AGI on which taxes will be determined, take the smallest amount of the following:

(A) 50% of excess over 1st level + 35% of excess over 2nd level	$21,300 (0.5 × $30,000) + (0.35 × $18,000)
(B) 85% of total benefits	$17,000 (0.85 × $20,000)
(C) 50% of total benefits + 85% of excess over 2nd level	$25,300 (0.5 × $20,000) + (0.85 × $18,000)

Source: 2009 Mercer Guide to Social Security.

In this example, Option B is smallest. Income taxes will be calculated based on a new AGI of $67,000 ($50,000 + $17,000). So $17,000 (85 percent) of Social Security benefits will be taxed.

Is Social Security a Balance-Sheet Asset?

The Social Security benefit should be treated as an income stream reducing the need to take the risks required to achieve your financial goal. By reducing the need to take risk (by the amount of the benefit), the allocation to less risky fixed income assets can be increased and required allocation to riskier equity asset classes reduced. All pensions can be treated in the same way.

File and Suspend Strategy

The SSA offers three types of benefits for retired workers and their spouses:

- **Retirement Worker Benefit (RWB)**—basic benefit determined by how long and how much an individual earns;
- **Spousal Benefit**—benefit provided to a worker's spouse once the worker has claimed his/her own benefit. This can be up to 50 percent of the spouse's full RWB or PIA;
- **Survivor Benefit**—benefit provided to surviving spouse after worker's death.

Using a File and Suspend strategy entitles the lower-earning spouse to a spousal benefit of up to 50 percent of the higher earning spouse's PIA. Additionally, the higher earner continues to work (or withdraw income elsewhere) to receive higher Social Security benefits at a later date, say age seventy. The File and Suspend strategy requires the higher-earning spouse to file at full retirement age (FRA) and immediately suspend benefits. This can be done at filing in the remarks section of the application, either on paper or online.

This strategy also benefits the couple in other ways. Should the higher earner die first, the surviving spouse would be entitled to a larger survivor benefit: the higher earner's delayed benefit. Essentially, the surviving spouse would get a step-up in benefits to 100 percent of the spouse's delayed benefit. By delaying benefits, the couple could also begin to draw down on the IRA for supplemental income. This both reduces the balance of the IRA and future required minimum distributions (RMDs) and can minimize the amount of future Social Security benefits that will be taxed.

Here's an example (see Table 15.2) in which the husband is the higher earner. The husband is sixty-six, his wife sixty-five. Using the file and suspend strategy, the husband files and suspends his benefits at age sixty-six ($2,000 per month). His wife files for half of her husband's PIA ($1,000 = $2,000 × 50 percent) at her FRA (or earlier but with a reduced benefit). The husband continues to work and draw additional income from his IRA to reduce future RMDs and delay claiming social security until age seventy. At age seventy, his monthly benefits will be $2,640. Should the husband die first, the wife would get a step-up in benefits, receiving the survivor benefit of $2,640 instead of $2,000 (had the husband filed and claimed benefits at his FRA).

If the husband dies at age eighty-three and the wife at eighty-five, the two Social Security income streams would look like this:

Table 15.2   File and Suspend

	Both claim at 66 (FRA)	File & suspend (until 70)
Husband benefit at 66 (FRA)	$2,000	N/A
Spousal benefit at 66 (FRA)	$1,000	$1,000
Husband benefit at 70	N/A	$2,640
Survivor benefit	$2,000	$2,640
Total SS benefits received (1)	$732,000	$871,920
Net present value of total SS benefits received (2)	$590,422	$683,521

(1) Calculations do not take into consideration taxes, COLA adjustments, or present value assumptions

(2) Calculations do not take into consideration taxes or COLA adjustments. Uses TIPS yield with maturity equal to life expectancy to discount cash flows through life expectancy as of February 25, 2009.

In summary, the File and Suspend strategy potentially allows for:

- The higher-earning spouse to delay benefits in order to receive a payment of up to 32 percent higher than the PIA.
- The lower earning spouse to become eligible for the spousal benefit before the higher-earning spouse begins taking claims.
- The lower-earning spouse to receive a larger survivor benefit equal to what the higher-earning spouse was receiving or entitled to.
- The reduction of RMDs by taking withdrawals from IRAs when needed prior to claiming benefits at age seventy, potentially keeping more Social Security benefits tax-free.

Due to longer life expectancies for women, this strategy works best for couples in good health where the husband was the higher income earner. If one of the spouses is in poor health or there is an immediate need for income, benefits should not be delayed. Alternatively, if there is a need to preserve the IRA because valuations are down and withdrawals should be delayed, Social Security benefits could be taken early. While the husband should wait to take delayed benefits, the wife can take benefits early and not significantly reduce the total amount of benefits the couple will

receive. To determine the best strategy on optimizing lifetime benefits, call the SSA and find out what each spouse's estimated benefits
will be at age sixty-two, sixty-six (or FRA), and seventy.

Double Dipping Strategy

Qualified nongovernmental workers can elect both a spousal benefit and worker benefit at different points in time during retirement:
the "double dipping" strategy. This strategy most benefits married
couples where both spouses have had similar lifetime earnings, but
it can be applied to any dual-income couple.

 If an individual qualifies for both benefits at the time of filing,
the Social Security office will assume the claimant is filing for both
benefits simultaneously. In that case, the individual will only receive
the higher of the two benefits. To prevent this, you need to clearly
state on the application which benefits are being claimed.

 While an individual can elect to take the retirement worker benefit (RWB) any time after age sixty-two, the spousal benefit can only
be taken after the spouse files for benefits. Furthermore, in order
to "double dip," an individual must file for the spousal benefit at
FRA in order to take their own RWB at a later date.

 Which benefit to claim first primarily depends on the actual
amount of each benefit. The amounts depend on how much the individual and their spouse earned and the ages at which they decide to
claim. Let's take a case where a married couple, John and Mary (both
sixty-two years old), have the following monthly social security benefits
(see Table 15.3):

Table 15.3   Double Dipping

	62	FRA	70
John's RWB	$1,600	$2,000	$2,640
Mary's RWB	$880	$1,100	$1,452
Mary's spousal	$700	$1,000	n/a

 Filing for a spousal benefit would entitle Mary to a benefit of
$1,000 at FRA. On reaching age seventy, Mary could then file for
her own RWB, increasing her benefit to $1,452.

 Double dipping is not gender-specific: Whichever spouse is the
lower-income earner can employ the strategy. If the spouses are
close in age, both can take advantage of double dipping. Note that

while the SSA allows this strategy, not all SSA officers are familiar with it. Be sure you talk to your Social Security benefits adviser prior to filing to clearly plan out your Social Security claiming strategy.

Summary

Individual circumstances drive the decision on when and how to take Social Security benefits. For those having the financial flexibility to defer benefits, higher annual benefits and other potential benefits like higher spousal and survivor benefits and longevity insurance generally make it more beneficial to defer. You may want to consult with a financial adviser or at least call the SSA and find out what you and your spouse's estimated benefits will be at age sixty-two, sixty-six (or FRA), and seventy.

CHAPTER 16

Determining a Safe Withdrawal Rate

In traditional retirement, planning the annual investment return is assumed to be a constant number, such as 8.5 percent per annum. This number depends on the asset allocation and on assumptions about the returns of the different asset classes. The outcome of the computation is typically presented as the expected wealth values over the anticipated period of retirement.

The problem with this approach is that investment returns are neither known nor constant over time. While investing is about risk, retirement calculators presenting single scenarios treat risk either as a certainty, or at best, as a 50/50 proposition: 50/50 you will do better or worse than the expected outcome. Investing is not an exact science; no one knows the precise return of different asset classes over any given number of years. Investment returns are random variables, characterized by expected values (or averages), standard deviations, and, more generally, probability distributions. For this reason, projections of an investment program's possible results should also be expressed in terms of probabilities. For example:

- There is a 95 percent chance you won't run out of money in retirement.
- There is a 50 percent probability you will accumulate at least $3.1 million. There is a 25 percent chance you will have $5.2 million or more. But there is also a 10 percent chance you will have $400,000 or less.

To arrive at these types of conclusions it is necessary to use what are known as Monte Carlo (MC) simulations.

Monte Carlo (MC) Simulations

MC simulations require a set of assumptions regarding time horizon, initial investment, asset allocation, withdrawals, savings, retirement income, rate of inflation, and correlation among the different asset classes.

In MC simulation programs, the growth of an investment portfolio is determined by two important inputs: portfolio average expected return and portfolio volatility, represented by the standard deviation measure. Based on these two inputs, the MC simulation program generates a sequence of random returns from which one return is applied in each year of the simulation. This process is repeated thousands of times to calculate the likelihood of possible outcomes and their potential distributions.

MC simulations also provide another important benefit: They allow investors to view the outcomes of various strategies and how marginal changes in asset allocations, savings rates and withdrawal rates change the odds of these outcomes.

For example, after examining the output, an investor might decide she is taking more risk than needed to achieve her goals. It's a relatively easy fix: lowering the equity allocation and/or lowering the exposure to risky asset classes. If she is not taking enough risk to provide acceptable odds of success, the decisions get more difficult. She must (1) take more risk than she would otherwise like to take, (2) lower the goal, (3) save more (lowering her current lifestyle), or (4) or accept and live with the estimated risk of failure.

The benefits of using an MC simulation are seen in this example. Assume the input results in an 80 percent chance of success (not running out of money while still alive). The simulation shows the impact on those odds of increasing (or decreasing) savings by $X a month. If that change increased the odds of success to 85 percent, the investor might decide that it is worthwhile to reduce current consumption to improve the odds of success by that amount. If it only raised the odds of success to 81 percent, the investor might draw a different conclusion.

The output can also be analyzed to see how changes in the asset allocation impact the odds of success. If increasing the equity allocation from 70 to 80 percent increased the odds of success from 80 to 90 percent, an investor might decide it was worth the extra risk of more equity ownership (and the extra stomach acid it was likely to produce along the way). If it only increased the odds of success to 81 percent, there might be a different decision. Changes in withdrawal rates that impact future lifestyle can be analyzed. For example, if a 4 percent withdrawal rate produced a 95 percent chance of success, and a 5 percent withdrawal rate lowered the odds of success to 90 percent, an investor might choose to raise the withdrawal rate, accepting a somewhat lower likelihood of success in return for greater consumption. If that decision is made and the risks do materialize, the investor must be prepared to accept an even lower lifestyle in the future.

The simulation program can be used to look at how delaying retirement by X years impacts various issues, such as the need to save, the withdrawal rate, or the required equity allocation. The same analysis can be done for earlier retirement. Investors can determine if an extra year of working is worth the greater lifestyle now and/or in the future, or how that extra year of work impacts the need to take risk. For example, each extra year of work might allow for a reduced need to save $X per year, a Y percent increase in the withdrawal rate, or a reduction in the equity allocation of Z percent.

The right answers are unique to the individual and their ability, willingness, and need to take risk. For some people, an 85 percent chance of running out of money will be perfectly acceptable. For others, anything short of 99 percent might be unacceptable. The decisions are all preferences driven by personal choice. Here are some guidelines:

- The more risk averse the investor, or the lower the marginal utility of wealth, the more emphasis should be placed on the odds of not running out of money rather than those of creating a large portfolio.
- Lower odds of success can be tolerated the more options an investor is both able and willing to exercise if the risks do "show up."

In the following examples applying the above principles, we will consider two investors, identical with one exception.

Application: The exception: one investor owns a second home. This investor has the ability to sell that home should the "left tail" (worst-case result) of the potential distribution of returns show up, so he can accept lower odds of not running out of money than the other investor. However, if the investor is unwilling to exercise that option—the grandchildren live in that area and a high value is placed on owning the property—the option doesn't matter. Only the options that investors are both able and willing to exercise should be considered.

Application: The exception: one investor is both willing and able to lower his need for cash flow from the portfolio should the "left tail" of the potential distribution of returns show up. That investor can accept lower odds of not running out of money more than one who is either unable or unwilling to lower his spending requirements.

Application: The exception: one investor is both willing and able to extend her planned time in the work force. The other places a higher value on her ability to retire. The investor who is both willing and able to continue to work longer can accept more risk, but she should consider the need for disability insurance should health prevent her from exercising the option to work longer.

Application: The exception: one investor has a long-term care policy. This investor can accept more investment risks than an investor without a policy.

Summary

The MC simulator can add significant value in the financial-planning process. In many, if not most cases, it is hard to see how one can make informed decisions without using this tool.

Our firm uses the Wagner RSP3 program to perform MC simulations.

In the Absence of an MC Simulator

If you do not have access to MC simulators, it is still possible to estimate an appropriate safe rate of withdrawal. Financial planners and investment advisers often use "the 4 percent rule." The rule comes from the study "Retirement 'Spending': Choosing a Sustainable Withdrawal Rate."[1] The authors found that a portfolio of 50 percent stocks and 50 percent bonds had a 95 percent historical success rate for a thirty-year horizon when using a 4 percent withdrawal rate, increasing that rate with inflation. Because the three finance professors who authored the study were from Trinity University, it is often referred to as the "Trinity Study."

The success or failure of your retirement spending plan mainly depends on three things: time horizon, spending amount, and the returns of your investment portfolio. The good news is that you have some control over all three. The bad news is that you are not in complete control over any of them.

The time horizon of your retirement is a function of your retirement age and life expectancy. Most people have at least some control over their retirement age. As for spending, you may have some discretionary spending. While you cannot control investment returns, you can decide on an asset allocation giving you the expected return required to support your needs.

Table 16.1 addresses time horizon by looking at mortality statistics. The percentages shown are the probability an individual at age sixty-five will survive to a particular age. The table is from a great resource on retirement planning issues, Moshe Milevsky's *Are You a Stock or a Bond?*

Table 16.1   Mortality Table at Age Sixty-Five

To Age:	Female (%)	Male (%)
70	94	92
75	85	81
80	72	66
85	56	46
90	35	24
95	16	8

Source: RP2000 Mortality Table, IFID Centre Calculations.

Table 16.1 can be a useful resource when planning the length of your retirement. An individual's personal health situation must also be taken into account when estimating the time horizon. Because the cost of being alive without sufficient assets to support an acceptable lifestyle is so high, we prefer to err on the side of a longer than necessary time horizon. For most retirees, leaving a larger estate than planned is preferable to running out of money in the last years of life and being forced to rely on relatives or selling a home.

The Safe Withdrawal Rate

Table 16.2 is a guideline for establishing a safe withdrawal rate. The results are based on our MC simulation work. The table summarizes the results at different ages for an individual whose equity allocation ranges from 30 to 50 percent. For those in the early phase of retirement we typically plan through age ninety.

Table 16.2   Monte Carlo Simulation Results

Age	Safe Withdrawal Rate (%)
55	3
60	4
65	4
70	5
75	6
80	7
85	8
90	9

Based on this table, a fifty-five-year-old should not take more than an inflation-adjusted 3 percent per annum from his portfolio. Thus, an individual with a portfolio of $1 million should not withdraw more than 30,000 the first year. He can adjust that amount each year for inflation. The table demonstrates that as time passes—and the horizon shortens—the safe withdrawal-rate percentage increases.

When using Table 16.2 to make withdrawal rate decisions, keep in mind it is not a "one size fits all" solution. If your health is such that you are likely to live well beyond age ninety or die much sooner than ninety, you should adjust your withdrawal rate accordingly. Those with other options to exercise (reduce discretionary spending, access home equity) can be more aggressive when choosing a withdrawal rate. Those without such options should consider a slightly more conservative withdrawal rate than the table indicates. The withdrawal rates shown are no guarantee a portfolio will not be depleted: They only indicate a high likelihood it will not occur.

Having decided on the appropriate withdrawal rate, you should choose the most tax-efficient location from which to make the withdrawals.

The Sequencing of Withdrawals to Fund Retirement

As discussed in Chapter 10, proper location of assets is an important part of the winning investment strategy. Another is using the most tax efficient withdrawal sequence to fund retirement. Should a retiree first withdraw funds from the taxable account, then the traditional IRA [401(k), 403(b), and other tax-deferred accounts], and finally the Roth IRA? Would another sequence be preferable? Two studies, Stephen M. Horan's "Withdrawal Location with Progressive Tax Rates"[2] and William Reichenstein's "Tax-Efficient Sequencing Of Accounts to Tap in Retirement"[3] provide answers.

The solutions are based on two key principles. The first: "Returns on funds held in Roth IRAs and traditional IRAs grow effectively tax exempt, while funds held in taxable accounts are usually taxed at positive effective tax rates." The second principle, discussed in Chapter 14, is that only "part of a traditional IRA's principal belongs to the investor. The IRS 'owns' the remaining portion. The objective is to minimize the government's share of the principal."[4]

Since the winning strategy is withdrawing funds from the account with the higher tax rate, the general rule of thumb is to first withdraw from taxable accounts. In addition, since we want to fund expenses with the most tax-inefficient assets, the sequencing of withdrawals from taxable accounts should first be from fixed income (bond) holdings. There are some exceptions to these rules:

- *The main source of income is derived from tax-sheltered accounts.* Withdrawals should be made from these accounts until taxable income at least reaches the lowest tax bracket. This exception should apply to any year when taxable income is low. For example, a retiree will likely be in a low tax bracket in years when she has large medical expenses, perhaps due to a stay in a nursing home.[5] For retirees with large balances (several million) in their IRAs, it may be appropriate to withdraw from those accounts until income reaches the 28 percent bracket.[6]
- *The beneficiaries of the IRA will be in a higher tax bracket than the owner.*

- *Retirees who have substantial unrealized gains on taxable assets can await the step-up in basis at death.* Such retirees should withdraw funds from retirement accounts before liquidating the appreciated asset. An example would be a terminally ill person, because the effective tax rate on the capital gains will be zero if they await the step-up in basis at death.
- *By delaying withdrawals from an IRA, the greater required minimum distributions (RMD) will cause the tax rate to rise to higher levels.* In addition, if a retiree is in a low tax bracket but doesn't need to withdraw funds from the IRA to meet spending needs, she should consider a conversion to a Roth IRA. Thus, the conventional wisdom to delay withdrawals from traditional IRAs for as long as possible is not always correct.

Traditional IRA versus Roth IRA

Many individuals face the decision of whether to withdraw from a traditional IRA or a Roth IRA. According to Reichenstein:

> Withdrawing funds from the traditional IRA makes sense in years when the retiree is in a low tax bracket and if the retiree's beneficiary will be in a higher tax bracket. Withdrawing funds from a Roth IRA instead of a traditional IRA makes sense in years when the retiree is in a high tax bracket and if the retiree's beneficiary will be in a lower tax bracket. In addition, Roth IRA withdrawals may also be preferred if the retiree expects to have large deductible medical expenses later in retirement—if the deductions lead to low tax rates. Withdrawals from a Roth may also be preferred if the retiree wishes to leave funds to a charity.[7]

Sensitivity Analysis

Reichenstein found that sequencing strategies are sensitive to the following:

- The higher the tax rate, the greater the advantage in first withdrawing from a taxable account. If capital gains taxes were increased the advantage would increase, as it would if an investor held an actively managed mutual fund that, due to turnover, was tax inefficient.

- The relative advantage of the "taxable account first" strategy is greatest when the portfolio is roughly evenly divided between retirement accounts and taxable accounts.
- The relative advantage of the taxable first strategy increases with the asset's rate of return.[8]

Summary

The academic literature suggests it is important to fund retirement spending in the right sequence. Monte Carlo simulations demonstrate that doing so will allow your financial portfolio to last a few years longer. Before any strategy is implemented, consult your tax adviser.

17

Planning Beyond Your Lifetime

Developing a well-designed investment policy statement is a necessary condition for successful financial planning. Besides addressing risk management issues, the overall financial plan should also integrate estate planning. We will briefly address this issue.

Estate Planning

Although not directly related to investing, estate planning is a key step in the overall planning process. Unfortunately, most people spend more time planning their next vacation than planning their estate. This isn't surprising, since vacations have near-term benefits and are more enjoyable to look forward to than our own demise. However, an estate plan is a critical step both to make sure your intentions are carried out after you are gone and to make tying up your affairs less stressful for your heirs.

An estate plan is important no matter your net worth. When putting it together, be mindful of federal and state laws governing estate issues. The first step is taking stock of your investments and insurance policies and deciding who you want to inherit different parts of your estate. The next step is drafting a will. If your affairs are complex, an estate-planning attorney would be a worthwhile investment. Working with your accountant and investment adviser, the attorney can help guide you through many other issues arising in the estate-planning process, including items such as the use of a trust, durable powers of attorney, estate taxes, and charitable giving. Also, discussing your estate plans with your heirs avoids surprises and conflicts after you are gone.

Recommended Reading

Whether or not you hire an attorney, a great resource for learning about estate planning is attorney Denis Clifford's book *Plan Your Estate.*

Preparing Your Heirs

Napoleon Bonaparte is widely regarded as one of the greatest military commanders, his campaigns studied at military academies all over the world. Yet he developed few military innovations. Perhaps the greatest contributor to his military success is summed up in a quotation usually attributed to him: "Most battles are won or lost long before the first shot is fired."

Each year, Americans spend billions of dollars preparing their assets for transition to their heirs. They engage high-powered estate and tax planners who set up complex vehicles like family limited partnerships, life insurance trusts, charitable remainder trusts, and charitable lead trusts. Despite these efforts, it is estimated that "70 percent of estates lose their assets and family harmony following the transition of the estate."[1] Given the talent engaged, it doesn't seem likely that failure is due to poor design. So why do most plans fail?

According to Roy Williams and Vic Preisser, authors of the *Estate Planning for the Post-Transition Period*, "The major causes of post-transition failures were discovered to lie within the family."[2] Estate plans failed mainly because the heirs were unprepared, didn't trust each other, and communications broke down. While the family and its advisers give great attention to preparing the assets for transition to the heirs, little if any attention is paid to preparing the heirs for the assets they will inherit.

What Do Parents Worry About Most?

Consider this list of the five things parents worry about most regarding wealth and its effect on their children:[3]

1. Too much emphasis on material things.
2. Naiveté about the value of money.

3. Spending beyond their means.
4. Initiative being ruined by affluence.
5. Will not do as well as parents would like.

Juxtapose these concerns with the typical focus of estate planning on taxation, preservation of wealth, and governance—not on any transfer of family values. There is an obvious disconnect. It's no surprise most plans fail.

Are Your Heirs Prepared for Their Assets?

To help determine if your heirs are prepared for their assets, Williams and Preisser suggest you ask yourself:

- Do your children (and their spouses) know your estate plan?
- Have they read your will?
- Do they know the family's net worth, meaning both yours and theirs (if they have assets in their name)?
- Are they in communication with your team of advisers (your attorney, accountant, and financial/investment adviser)?

Two more important questions: Have the children been involved in the formation of the investment policy statement, and are they familiar with the investment strategy, goals, and how to manage the assets?

Taboo Topic

Families often treat money and the issues surrounding wealth as taboo subjects. These "lessons" of noninvolvement get passed on from one generation to the next, explaining why failure rates are so high. The solution: Treat family wealth as a private matter, but not private within the family.

Those Who Fail to Plan, Plan to Fail

For a plan to be successful, Williams and Preisser recommend that heirs, including spouses, should have some influence on how the estate is structured. At the very least, they should have input. There should be a plan to prepare them for their future responsibilities and thought given to whether the estate plan matches their skills and interests. Heirs should know the impact of their wealth on their family and the responsibilities of wealth.

A transition plan should include a family wealth mission statement addressing these issues:[4]

1. The overall purpose of the family's wealth and a strategy to implement it, with roles well defined;
2. Entire family participation in the important decisions;
3. Options for family members to participate in asset management;
4. Heirs understanding and buying into their roles;
5. Heirs reviewing and understanding all documents;
6. Asset distributions based on readiness, not age of heirs;
7. Incentives and opportunities for heirs;
8. Encouraging younger children to participate in philanthropic decisions;
9. Family unity as an important asset;
10. Open, regular family communication.

Benefits of Creating a Family Wealth Mission Statement (FWMS)

The FWMS has a multitude of benefits, beginning with articulating why it exists and why you have chosen to manage and distribute your estate in a particular manner. It should identify how the wealth was achieved, the life experiences shaping your financial philosophy, what wealth means to you, how it is important to you, and, most importantly, the values you wish to pass on.

The process of creating a FWMS helps identify and examine the people and entities held in the highest esteem, leading to wealth transfer decisions that make the most sense. As a clear expression for heirs and others, the FWMS can be a tool to help pass on personal values to future generations: identifying those charities or organizations for which you feel the most passion and desire to support with your social capital, as well as the individuals for whom you feel responsible and why you feel an obligation to give them a portion of your wealth.

The FWMS succinctly informs all advisers of your intentions, saving both time and money as they explore appropriate strategies to help you achieve your wishes. It should specifically identify how much money is needed during your lifetime and how much you wish to leave to your heirs. It should also identify why you believe the amounts are appropriate and what you want to achieve by giving them money.

Finally, the FWMS document should be signed and dated to demonstrate it is a valid document and accurately reflects your wishes.

In summary, just as most battles are won in the preparatory stage, the success of a family wealth transition plan depends on the effort and emphasis placed on transitioning not only the family's wealth but the family's values.

Recommended Reading

To learn more about this subject, read the aforementioned *Estate Planning for the Post-Transition Period, Preparing Heirs* and *For Love & Money*. All three are by Roy O. Williams and Vic Preisser.

Conclusion

We hope this book has met its goals of helping you:

- Design an Investment Policy Statement (IPS) and asset allocation plan most appropriate to your unique situation.
- Choose the best investment vehicles to implement the plan.
- Locate assets in the most tax-efficient manner.
- Maintain the portfolio's risk profile in the most efficient manner.
- Provide effective tax management.
- Integrate into your investment plan estate planning, tax planning, risk management (insurance of all kinds), and planning for your heirs.

Larry adds this: I have greatly enjoyed the thousands of e-mails and letters I have received over the years from readers of my books. If you have any questions about this book or how to implement the recommended strategies, feel free to contact me at Buckingham Asset Management, 8182 Maryland Avenue, Suite 900, Clayton, Missouri 63105, or e-mail me at lswedroe@bamstl.com. You can also e-mail Kevin Grogan at kgrogan@bamstl.com or Tiya Lim at tlim@bamstl.com.

APPENDIX A

Effective Diversification in a Three-Factor World

In their June 1992 *Journal of Finance* article, "The Cross-Section of Expected Stock Returns," professors Eugene F. Fama and Kenneth R. French revolutionized the way many individuals think about investing. Prior to the study, the prevailing theory (known as the "capital asset pricing model" or CAPM) was that the risk and return of a portfolio was largely determined by one factor: its beta. Beta is a measure of equity-type risk (or market risk) of a stock, mutual fund, or portfolio, relative to the risk of the overall U.S. stock market. An asset with a beta greater than one has more equity-type risk than the overall market; one with a beta less than one has less equity-type risk than the overall market.

The authors demonstrated we actually live in a three-factor world. The risk and return of a portfolio is also explained by its exposure to two other risk factors: size and price. Fama and French hypothesized that while small-cap and value stocks have higher beta—more equity-type risk—they also have *additional* risk unrelated to beta. Thus, small-cap and value stocks are riskier than large-cap and growth stocks, explaining their higher historical returns and implying such stocks should have higher expected returns in the future. Studies have confirmed that the three-factor model explains an overwhelming majority of the returns of diversified portfolios.

Using the Fama-French data series for the period 1927–2008, the average annual returns to these three risks factors were:

- **Market Factor** (the return of the all-equity universe minus the return on one-month Treasury bills): 7.5 percent.
- **Size Factor** (the return of small-cap stocks minus the return of large-cap stocks): 3.0 percent.
- **Price Factor** (the return of high book-to-market [value] stocks minus the return of low book-to-market [growth] stocks): 5.0 percent.

Independent Risk Factors

Size and price are independent (unique) risk factors in that they provide investors with exposure to different risks than those provided by exposure to market risks. Evidence of this independence can be seen when we examine the historical correlations of the size and price factors to the market factor. High correlations would mean the risk factors would be relatively good substitutes for each other. If that were the case, while investors could increase the expected return (and risk) of the portfolio by increasing their exposure to these risk factors, there would be no real diversification benefit. If the correlations are low, investors could both increase expected returns for a given level of risk and gain a diversification benefit.

For the period 1927–2008, the correlation of the market risk factor to the size risk factor was .38, and its correlation to the price risk factor .11. The correlation of the size risk factor to the price risk factor was almost zero (.04). In other words, one can effectively diversify equity risks by diversifying across the three independent risk factors. Each risk factor has the potential for increasing investment returns. Two recent examples demonstrate that size and price are independent risk factors.

- In 2001, small-cap stocks returned 18.0 percent and small-cap value stocks 40.6 percent, while large-cap stocks produced a negative return of 12.7 percent.
- In 1998, while large-cap stocks rose 27.0 percent, small-cap stocks fell 2.3 percent and small-cap value stocks fell 10.0 percent.

Diversifying Risk

In the one-factor world, there seemed to be only two ways to increase returns: increase the allocation to stocks or buy higher beta stocks. In either case, investors were taking more of exactly the same type of risk they were already taking. The Fama and French research indicated other ways to increase the expected return of a portfolio. Instead of adding more of the same type of risk, investors could add different types of risk to achieve more effective diversification. The following simplified example (which ignores the diversification return) will illustrate this point.

Assume we expect equities to provide a future annualized return of 7 percent, and we have current bond yields of about 5 percent. Consider a portfolio that is 50 percent bonds and 50 percent stocks. This allocation results in an expected portfolio return of 6 percent. If the portfolio's objective is to achieve a return of 6.5 percent, one way to increase the expected return is to increase the allocation to stocks from 50 percent to 75 percent.

$$(75\% \times 7\%) + (25\% \times 5\%) = 6.5\%$$

Now consider an alternative strategy, one diversifying risk to other risk factors. For the period 1927–2008, small-cap value stocks achieved an annualized return of 13.0 percent, 3.5 percent higher than the market's annualized return of 9.5 percent. Further assume that same relationship will continue in the future. If we hypothetically forecast market returns of 7 percent, we would also forecast that small-cap value stocks would return 10.5 percent. Using this information, we can look at the expected returns for a few different portfolio allocations.

First, consider a portfolio taking half of the equities and allocating them to small-cap value stocks. The expected return would now be:

$$(25\% \times 7\%) + (25\% \times 10.5\%) + (50\% \times 5\%) = 6.875\%$$

By increasing the allocation to riskier stocks we increased the expected return—and the risk of the portfolio. As the result might be more risk than the investor has the ability, willingness, or need to take, let's consider another alternative. This time, while shifting some of the equity allocation to small-cap value stocks (increasing risk), we also lower the overall equity allocation to just 40 percent (lowering risk). The new allocations are 20 percent total market index, 20 percent small-cap value stocks, and 60 percent bonds. The expected return would now be:

$$(20\% \times 7\%) + (20\% \times 10.5\%) + (60\% \times 5\%) = 6.5\%$$

We now have a portfolio with a 40 percent allocation to stocks with the same expected return as the portfolio having a 75 percent allocation to stocks. But in this case, instead of increasing the expected return by taking more of the same type of risk (market risk), we increased returns by adding different types of risk: the risk factors of small-cap and value stocks. We diversified our equity risks across these two independent factors. This is a more effective form of diversification. While the expected returns of the two portfolios are the same, their risks are different.

Risk Aversion

There is another consideration especially important to risk-averse investors (which most are). Since bonds are safer investments than stocks in a severe bear market the portfolio's maximum loss would likely be far lower with a 40 percent equity allocation than with a 75 percent one. Thus, while the expected returns of the two portfolios are the same, the portfolio with the lower equity allocation has less downside risk. Of course, the upside potential during a strong bull market is correspondingly lower. For an investor for whom the pain of a loss is greater than the benefit of an equal-sized gain, reducing downside risk at the price of reducing upside potential is a good trade-off.

Considerations

Several factors should be given careful consideration when deciding on the appropriate portfolio mix. First, as discussed in Chapter 3, an investor should consider how his or her labor capital correlates with the greater economic cycle risks of small-cap and value stocks compared to large-cap and growth stocks.

The second consideration is a psychological one: tracking error regret. Recall, tracking error is the amount by which the performance of a portfolio varies from that of the total market or other broad market benchmark, such as the S&P 500 Index. By diversifying across risk factors, investors take on increased tracking error risk. While very few investors care when tracking error is positive (their portfolio beats the benchmark), many care when it's negative.

To have a chance for positive tracking error, investors must accept the likelihood negative tracking error will appear from time to time, or there would be no risk. Emotions associated with negative tracking error can lead many investors to abandon carefully developed investment plans. Only those investors willing and able to accept tracking error risk should consider diversifying across the other risk factors.

Summary

Fama and French identified two additional risk factors you should consider when constructing portfolios. You can either use those risk factors to try to increase the *expected* return (and risk) of a portfolio, or maintain the expected return of the portfolio by diversifying across them while lowering the equity allocation. For many investors, we believe diversifying across these independent risk factors is a more effective way to diversify portfolio risk.

If you consider this strategy, remember that just as the equity premium is compensation for taking risk, so are the size and value premiums. Thus, we add the usual "disclaimer": The future may look different from the past.

APPENDIX B

Dollar Cost Averaging

Investors frequently face this kind of issue: "I just received a large lump sum of money. Should I invest it all at once, or spread the investment out over time?" A similar problem arises when an investor has sold during a bear market. The question then is: How do you reenter the market?

Rather than investing assets in a lump sum, many investors use dollar cost averaging (DCA), a timing strategy that periodically invests a fixed amount of money in a particular investment or portfolio over a given time interval. The idea is to lower the total average cost per share of the investment, giving the investor a lower overall cost for the shares purchased over time. Such is the theory. But is there any real advantage to using DCA as an investment strategy?

From an academic perspective, answering the question of when to invest is simple and has been known for a long time. The June 1979 issue of the *Journal of Financial and Quantitative Analysis* published an article by University of Chicago professor George Constantinides titled, "A Note on the SubOptimality of Dollar Cost Averaging as an Investment Policy." Constantinides showed DCA to be an inferior strategy to lump sum investing. In 1992, John Knight and Lewis Mandell published "Nobody Gains From Dollar Cost Averaging: Analytical, Numerical, and Empirical Results," in the *Financial Services Review* (Vol. 2, Issue 1). Knight and Mandell compared DCA to a buy and hold strategy, then analyzed the strategies across a series of investor profiles from risk averse to aggressive. The authors noted: "Brokerage firms endorse DCA for two reasons.

First, they state that returns are increased because more shares are purchased when prices are low and fewer when prices are high. Secondly, they assert that DCA enhances investor utility by preventing an ill-timed lump sum investment. Our results do not support either of these contentions." Knight and Mandell concluded: "Using three separate methods of comparison, we have shown the lack of any advantage of DCA relative to two alternative investment strategies. Our numerical trial and empirical evidence, in consonance with our graphical analysis, both favor optimal rebalancing and buy and hold strategies over dollar cost averaging."

Here is another way to think about DCA. Assume that staying fully invested in equities is suboptimal, meaning you should sell all your equities and then DCA back into the market. At the next investment period you have some money in the stock market already. While you planned to periodically reinvest in the market, you also determined that staying fully invested is suboptimal. You run into this difficulty: Do you continue to buy equities, sell your existing holdings, or do both? Logically, DCA cannot be effective.

Why Is DCA So Popular?

Despite the academic evidence, investors and advisers still recommend DCA. They argue that since markets are volatile, DCA allows investors to avoid investing too much when the market is priced high and too little when it's priced low, thus reducing overall market risk. However, they ignore the simple logic that since there is always an equity risk premium—stocks having higher expected returns than bonds—common sense tells us to invest all at once.

Investors and advisers do not always base decisions on logic or evidence. Emotions, such as fear, often play a far greater role in decision making.

When Does DCA Make Sense?

While DCA is not an optimal investment strategy, it has value when facing the "lesser of two evils," that is, when an investor simply cannot "take the plunge" and invest all at once for fear of what could happen to the stock market. Fear causes paralysis. If the market rises after they delay, they think, "How can I buy now at even higher prices?" If the market falls, "I can't buy now. That bear market I was afraid of is here." Once deciding not to buy, how do you decide to ever buy again?

One solution is to write down a plan laying out a schedule with regularly planned investments. The plan might include one of these alternatives:

- Invest one-third of the investment immediately and invest the remaining two-thirds in equal amounts over the next two months or next two quarters;
- Invest one-quarter today and spread the remainder equally over the next three quarters;
- Invest one-sixth each month for six months or every other month.

Having written up the schedule, the investor should sign the document. If working with an adviser, the adviser should be instructed to implement the plan, regardless of market performance. Otherwise, the latest headlines or guru forecasts might tempt the investor to stray from the plan.

If the market rises after the initial investment, the investor can feel good about how the portfolio has performed, and how smart she was not to delay investing. If it falls, the investor can feel good about the opportunity to buy at lower prices, and about being smart enough to not put all her money in at one time. From a psychological perspective it's a win/win. Since we know emotions play an important role in how individuals view outcomes, this is an important consideration.

Once convinced that a gradualist approach is the correct one, the investor should ask himself this question: "Having made my initial partial investment, do I want to see the market rise or fall?" The logical answer, and the one that will keep the investor sticking to the plan, is: "I want to see it fall. That way I can make my future investments at lower prices."

APPENDIX C

Reverse Mortgages

Retirees are often house rich but cash poor, their homes being their largest assets. There used to be just three significant ways to get equity from a home:

- Sell it;
- Rent it;
- Borrow against it using either a cash-out refinance or a home-equity loan.

Reverse mortgages present a fourth option, allowing homeowners to receive some of the home's equity without moving or making regular loan repayments. Reverse mortgages provide an alternative financing method (though an expensive one) that can help homeowners maintain their independence as well as an adequate standard of living.

People who take out reverse mortgages often:

- Have a regular need for additional funds;
- Live on a fixed income with their home equity as their most significant asset;
- Do not plan to leave their home to their heirs.

Reverse Mortgage Features

Reverse mortgages resemble conventional mortgages in that lenders pay homeowners based on the equity in the home. The biggest difference is that with a reverse mortgage homeowners do not immediately begin paying back the loan. Generally, the loans are not due until the home is no longer the homeowners' principal residence. Money received from reverse mortgages is not taxable and typically does not affect homeowners' other assets or their Medicare or Social Security benefits.

Borrowers can repay reverse mortgages with other assets but typically repay them by selling the home. Any equity remaining after selling the home belongs to the homeowners or their heirs. Most reverse mortgages have a nonrecourse clause, meaning the debt cannot be passed along to the estate or heirs.

The amount borrowers receive depends on several factors, including:

- Age;
- The current interest rate;
- Loan fees;
- The home's appraised value or the Federal Housing Administration's (FHA's) mortgage limits for the area, whichever is less.

Because the maximum amount available is partly dependent on age, the longer borrowers wait before taking out a reverse mortgage, the greater the amount available. Many reverse mortgages have no income restrictions. Generally, borrowing limits increase when there is more equity in the home, the borrowers are older, and interest rates are at low levels.

Loan Considerations

Reverse mortgages involve several costs: origination fees, other up-front closing costs, as well as service fees during the term of the mortgage. Private mortgage insurance may also be required.

The amount owed on reverse mortgages generally grows over time. Interest is charged on the outstanding balance and added each month. If the debt exceeds the value of the property, the FHA or lender would take the losses due to the nonrecourse nature of most reverse mortgages.

Interest rates on reverse mortgages can be either fixed or variable. Because borrowers retain the titles to their homes, they remain responsible for property taxes and all other homeowner expenses.

Failing to pay property taxes or maintain homeowners insurance puts borrowers at risk of the loan becoming due.

Eligible Property Types

The home must be a one-to-four unit property, which includes townhouses, detached or manufactured homes, and units in condominiums. Condominiums must be FHA-approved.

How Are Payments Received?

In addition to taking a lump-sum payment, borrowers have five options:

- **Tenure**—Indefinite equal monthly payments.
- **Term**—Equal monthly payments over a certain time period.
- **Line of credit**—A set amount borrowers can draw from whenever necessary.
- **Modified tenure**—Combination of line of credit and tenure.
- **Modified term**—Combination of line of credit and term.

Types of Reverse Mortgages

There are three types of reverse mortgages:

- Single-purpose reverse mortgages—Offered for a single purpose, such as home repairs.
- Home-equity conversion mortgages (HECMs)—Backed by the U.S. Department of Housing and Urban Development (HUD).
- Proprietary reverse mortgages—Loans developed and backed by private companies. Due to their complex nature and infinite variety, we will not cover them.

Single-Purpose Reverse Mortgages

Single-purpose reverse mortgages typically have the lowest costs of the different types of reverse mortgages. Usually, only borrowers with low or moderate income qualify for these loans.

HECMs

HECMs are the most popular type of reverse mortgage. The size of HECMs depends on the maximum loan limit, which varies by county and changes over time. As of 2010, due to changes enacted by the 2009 Stimulus Plan, the federal maximum was $625,500. Before applying for HECMs, borrowers must meet with a counselor from an independent government-approved housing counseling agency. During the meeting, the counselor must explain costs, financial implications, and alternatives.

HECMs tend to cost more compared to other home loans. For example, an HECM might involve not only a 2 percent origination fee, but also a 2 percent fee for mortgage insurance and a monthly service fee of 0.5 percent. By having insurance on reverse mortgages, homeowners can turn to the government for their loan funds should the company managing the account go under. Furthermore, the mortgage insurance guarantees that borrowers will never owe more than the value of the home when HECMs must be repaid.

Beware of High Up-Front Costs

Reverse mortgages carry high up-front costs compared to conventional home loans, though it is important to note that these costs (with the possible exception of an application fee) become part of the loan balance. The initial high costs make reverse mortgages prohibitively expensive for the short-term user. The National Center for Home Equity Conversion provides this example.[1] A 75-year-old single woman gets a $150,000 HECM on her home and finances $6,500 in up-front costs as part of the loan. She receives monthly advances of $562 indefinitely, and her home appreciates at 4 percent per year. If this reverse mortgage is paid off two years later, the loan's effective interest cost is almost 50 percent! She receives only $13,488 for the life of the loan, compared with $6,500 incurred as up-front costs (not counting accrued interest). She would receive $80,928 over the life of the loan if she stayed in the home for 12 years, driving the cost of the loan down to 10.8 percent.

The example demonstrates why reverse mortgages may be more risky for people needing in-home care. If their health condition requires moving into an assisted living or nursing home, the reverse mortgage stops making advances and the loan must be repaid, though some loans have a grace period before repayment starts.

Other Points

- HUD provides names of its approved lenders, and these lenders will help with the application and approval process at no cost.
- Although the proceeds are tax free, reverse mortgages may impact eligibility for certain need-based public benefits such as Medicaid or Supplemental Social Security Income.
- During periods of low interest rates, comfortably sustaining withdrawal rates of 3 – 4 percent from conservatively structured portfolios becomes harder to achieve. On the other hand, periods of low interest rates favor reverse mortgages because low initial rates result in larger payouts or monthly payments. Thus, reverse mortgages can supplement portfolio returns when interest rates are low or falling, and may also help individuals (and their advisers) resist the temptation to stretch for yield by extending maturities or lowering credit-quality standards.

Summary

While reverse mortgages can be a relatively expensive means of borrowing, they may be appropriate for some individuals, enabling them to maintain their homes, their independence, and an adequate standard of living. A significant advantage of reverse mortgages is that there are no income requirements—not the case with many other forms of financing.

APPENDIX D

How to Choose an Adviser You Can Trust

The objective of this book is to make you an informed investor. We have attempted to provide you with the information necessary to design and implement a prudent investment plan giving you the best chance of achieving your goals. There are investors who recognize they have neither the knowledge nor the discipline required to be successful on their own. They also recognize that a good financial adviser can add value in many ways. Other individuals would rather have someone else focus on financial matters so that they can focus more of their attention on important things in their lives: family, friends, community service, or hobbies. We offer the following advice for those thinking of employing a financial adviser.

When interviewing a financial advisory firm, have its representatives make the following twelve commitments to you. Doing so will give you the greatest chance of avoiding conflicts of interest and the greatest chance of achieving your financial goals.

1. The firm's guiding principle is that the advice provided will always be in your best interest.
2. The firm will provide a fiduciary standard of care: the highest legal duty one party can have to another.
3. The firm is a fee-only adviser, avoiding conflicts that commission-based compensation can create.
4. The firm fully discloses potential conflicts.

5. The advice is based on the latest academic research, not on opinions.
6. The firm is client centered: It doesn't sell products, only advice.
7. The firm provides a high level of personal attention: Each client is assigned a team of professionals with which they will develop strong personal relationships.
8. The firm's employees invest their personal assets, including their profit-sharing plan, based on the same set of investment principles and in the same or comparable securities they recommend.
9. The firm develops an investment plan that is integrated into estate, tax, and risk management (insurance) plans and tailored to your unique situation.
10. The firm meets with clients on a regular basis to review their plans and determine whether anything significant has changed that would cause the underlying assumptions upon which the plan was built to change. If there have been changes, the firm will adapt the plan to the new circumstances.
11. The firm's advice is always goal oriented, evaluating each decision not in isolation, but in terms of its impact on the likelihood of success of the *overall* plan.
12. The firm's comprehensive wealth management services are provided by individuals with CFA, CFP, PFS, or other comparable designations.

Good advice doesn't have to be expensive. However, bad or untrustworthy advice almost always costs dearly, no matter how little you pay for it. Perform a thorough due diligence before choosing a financial advisory firm. That due diligence should include both the twelve commitments and a careful review of form ADV, a disclosure document setting forth information about the adviser, including investment strategy, fee schedules, conflicts of interest, and regulatory incidents.

Notes

Chapter 2

1. *BusinessWeek*, September 16, 1996.

Chapter 3

1. Peter L. Bernstein and Aswath Damodaran, eds., *Investment Management*, (New York: John Wiley & Sons, 1998), p. 379.
2. David Laster, "Measuring Gains From International Equity Diversification: The Bootstrap Approach," *Journal of Investing* (Fall 1998).

Chapter 6

1. Dale L. Domain and William Reichenstein, "Returns-Based Style Analysis of High-Yield Bonds," *Journal of Fixed Income* (Spring 2008).
2. Gary Baierl, Robert Cummisford, Mark W. Riepe, and updated by James St. Aubin, "Investing in Global Hard Assets: A Diversification Tool for Portfolios," *Ibbotson Associates* (March 2005), p. 11.
3. Moshe A. Milevsky and Steven E. Posner, "The Titanic Option: Valuation of the Guaranteed Minimum Death Benefit in Variable Annuities and Mutual Funds," *The Journal of Risk and Insurance* (March 2001), p. 93.
4. Jeffrey Brown and James Poterba, "The Household Ownership of Variable Annuities," Working Paper (October 2005), p. 7.
5. Carolyn T. Geer, "The Great Annuity Rip-Off," *Forbes*, February 1998.

Chapter 7

1. Gene Amromin, Jennifer C. Huang, and Clemens Sialm, "Responsible Fools? The Tradeoff Between Mortgage Prepayments and Tax-Deferred Retirement Savings," March 15, 2006.

Chapter 9

1. Mark Carhart, "On Persistence in Mutual-Fund Performance," *Journal of Finance* (March 1997).

2. Russ Wermers, "Mutual-Fund Performance: An Empirical Decomposition into Stock-Picking Talent, Style, Transaction Costs, and Expenses," *Journal of Finance* (August 2000).

3. Rob Bauer, Rik Frehen, Hurber Lum, and Roger Otten, "The Performance of U.S. Pension Plans," April 3, 2007.

4. Amit Goyal and Sunil Wahal, "The Selection and Termination of Investment Management Firms by Plan Sponsors," May 2005.

5. Brad Barber and Terrance Odean, "Trading Is Hazardous to Your Wealth: The Common Stock Investment Performance of Individual Investors," *Journal of Finance* (April 2000).

6. Brad Barber and Terrance Odean, "Do Investors Trade Too Much?" *American Economic Review* (December 1999).

7. Brad Barber and Terrance Odean, "Too Many Cooks Spoil the Profit: The Performance of Investment Clubs," *Financial Analysts Journal* (January/February 2000).

8. Jonathan B. Berk, "Five Myths of Active Management."

9. Ibid.

10. Roger Edelen, Richard Evans, and Gregory B. Kadlec, "Scale Effects in Mutual Fund Performance: The Role of Trading Costs," March 17, 2007.

11. William Sherden, *The Fortune Sellers* (New York: John Wiley & Sons, 1998).

12. *Industry Week*, April 20, 1992, p. 76.

13. Dwight Lee and James Verbrugge, "The Efficient Market Theory Thrives on Criticism," *Journal of Applied Corporate Finance* (Spring 1996).

Chapter 13

1. David F. Babbel and Craig B. Merrill, "Rational Decumulation," Working Paper (July 2006).

2. Matthew Goldstein, "Why Death Bonds Look So Frail." *BusinessWeek*, February 14, 2008.

3. Stephan R. Leimberg, E. Randolph Whitelaw, Richard M. Weber and Liz Colosimo, "Life Settlements: Tax, Accounting, and Securities Law Issues. *Estate Planning*, September 2006."

4. Ibid.

5. Donald Jay Korn, "You Bet Your Life," *Financial Planning*, August 1, 2008.

6. Robert Powell, "It's Settled: Don't Use Life Settlements," *MarketWatch*, June 2, 2005.

7. "The Strange Saga of STOLI," *Kiplinger.com*, July 2008.

Chapter 16

1. Cooley, Phillip L., Carl M. Hubbard, and Daniel T. Walz, 1998. "Retirement 'Spending': Choosing a Sustainable Withdrawal Rate," *AAII Journal* 20: 16–21.

2. Stephen M. Horan, "Withdrawal Location with Progressive Tax Rates," *Financial Analysts Journal* (November–December 2006).

3. William Reichenstein, "Tax-Efficient Sequencing of Accounts to Tap in Retirement," Trends and Issues, TIAA-CREF Institute, October 2006.

4. Ibid.
5. Ibid.
6. Horan.
7. Reichenstein.
8. Ibid.

Chapter 17

1. Roy Williams and Vic Preisser, *Estate Planning for the Post-Transition Period.* Preview Copy, May 2007.
2. Ibid.
3. Ibid.
4. Ibid.

Appendix C

1. Reverse Mortgages Demystified. Available at http://www.help4srs.org/finance/reverse_mortgages.htm. Accessed May 21, 2010.

Sources of Data

Barclays Bank PLC for data on the Barclays Capital U.S. Intermediate Credit Bond Index. Barclays Capital and the Barclays Capital U.S. Intermediate Credit Bond Index are trademarks of Barclays Bank PLC.

Professor Kenneth R. French for data on risk premiums and stock market returns. Used with permission.

Morgan Stanley for data on the returns of the MSCI EAFE index. Used with permission. The information is the exclusive property of MSCI Inc. ("MSCI") and may not be reproduced or redisseminated in any form or used to create any financial products or indices without MSCI's prior written permission. This information is provided "as is" and none of MSCI, its affiliates or any other person involved in or related to the compilation of this information (collectively, the "MSCI Parties") makes any express or implied warranties or representations with respect to the information or the results to be obtained by the use thereof, and the MSCI Parties hereby expressly disclaim all implied warranties (including, without limitation, the implied warranties of merchantability and fitness for a particular purpose) with respect to this information. In no event shall any MSCI Party have any liability of any kind to any person or entity arising from or related to this information.

Morningstar for data on the returns of one-month Treasury bills, used to calculate the equity risk premium and the size and value premiums. Used with permission.

Standard and Poors for data on the returns of the S&P 500 Index. Used with permission.

The Center for Research in Security Prices at the University of Chicago for data on the U.S. stock market returns. The data is calculated or derived based on data from CRSP US Stock Database © 200905 Center for Research in Security Prices (CRSP®), Graduate School of Business, The University of Chicago, 200905 being the year and month the database was published. Used with permission.

Glossary

401(k) A defined contribution plan offered by a corporation to its employees that allows employees to set aside tax-deferred income for retirement purposes.

403(b) A retirement plan offered by nonprofit organizations, such as universities and charitable organizations, rather than corporations. Similar to a 401(k) plan.

Active management The attempt to uncover securities the market has either under- or overvalued and/or the attempt to time investment decisions to be more heavily invested when the market is rising and less so when the market is falling.

Agency risk The risk of loss due to an agent's/manager's pursuit of his own interests instead of those of the principals/investors.

AGI Adjusted gross income.

Alpha A measure of risk-adjusted performance relative to a benchmark. Positive alpha represents outperformance. Negative alpha represents underperformance. Positive or negative alpha may be caused by luck, manager skill, costs, and/or wrong choice of benchmark.

Alternative minimum tax (AMT) A tax originally targeted at a small number of high-income taxpayers who could claim so many deductions that they owed little or no income tax under the traditional tax code.

Annuitization The conversion of part or all of the assets in a qualified retirement plan or annuity contract into a stream of regular income payments.

Arbitrage The process by which investors exploit the price difference between two identical securities by simultaneously buying one at a lower price and selling the other at a higher price (thereby avoiding risk). This action locks in a risk-free profit for the arbitrageur (the one engaging in the arbitrage). The trading activity of arbitrageurs eventually eliminates these price differences.

Asset allocation The process of determining what percentage of assets should be dedicated to which specific asset classes. Also, the end result of this process.

Asset class A group of assets with similar risk and expected return characteristics. Cash, debt instruments, real estate, and equities are examples of asset classes. Within a major asset class, such as equities, there are more specific classes, such as large and small company stocks and domestic and international stocks.

Basis point One one-hundredth of 1 percent, or 0.0001.

Beginning value Value of the portfolio at the beginning of the reporting period.

Benchmark An appropriate standard against which mutual funds and other investment vehicles can be judged. Domestic large-cap growth funds should be judged against a large-cap growth index such as the S&P 500 Index, while small-cap managers should be judged against a small-cap index such as the Russell 2000 Index.

Bid-offer spread The bid is the price at which you can sell a security, and the offer is the price you must pay to buy a security. The spread is the difference between the two prices and represents the cost of a round-trip trade (purchase and sale), excluding commissions.

Book value An accounting concept reflecting the value of a company based on accounting principles. It is often expressed in per-share terms. Book value per share is equal to book equity divided by the number of shares.

Book-value-to-market value (BtM) The ratio of the book value per share to the market price per share, or book value divided by market capitalization.

Broker-dealer Any individual or firm in the business of buying and selling securities for itself and others. Broker-dealers must register with the SEC. When acting as a broker, a broker-dealer executes orders on behalf of his or her client. When acting as a dealer, a broker-dealer executes trades for his or her firm's own account. Securities bought for the firm's own account may be sold to clients or other firms, or they may become a part of the firm's holdings.

Call An option contract that gives the holder the right, but not the obligation, to buy a security at a predetermined price on a specific date (European call) or during a specific period (American call).

Call premium The percentage above the principal amount of a bond that is paid by the issuer when they call the bond.

Capital appreciation The increase or decrease in dollar value of all securities in the portfolio for a specified period.

Cash invested Dollar amount of all purchases not including reinvested dividends/interest/capital gains.

Closet index fund An actively managed fund whose holdings so closely resemble the holdings of an index fund that investors are unknowingly paying larger fees for minimal differentiation.

Coefficient of correlation A statistical term describing how closely the price movements of different securities or asset classes are related. The higher the coefficient, the stronger the relationship between price movements of the two securities/asset classes.

Collateralized commodity futures (CCF) Fully collateralized securities that invest in the commodity futures market with the collateral being a risk-free investment, typically a Treasury security.

Commercial paper Short-term, unsecured promissory notes issued primarily by corporations.

Commodity A physical good (such as corn, oil, or gold) that is supplied without significant qualitative differentiation.

Compensated risk Risk that cannot be diversified away (like the risk of owning stocks). The market rewards investors for accepting compensated risk with a risk premium (a greater *expected* return) commensurate with the amount of risk accepted.

Convertible Security that can be exchanged for a specified amount of another, related security at the option of the issuer or the holder.

Cost basis A tax computation used in determining capital gains. Cost basis is usually the original purchase price of shares owned, including all fees, plus the dollar amount of all reinvested dividends/interest/capital gains.

Consumer price index (CPI) A measure of price inflation.

CRSP The Center for Research in Security Prices is a financial research group at the University of Chicago business school.

Currency risk The risk that an investment's value will be affected by changes in exchange rates.

Current yield The ratio of the coupon rate on a bond to the current price expressed as a percentage. Thus, if you pay par, or one hundred cents on the dollar, for your bond, and the coupon rate is 6 percent, the current yield is 6 percent. If you pay 97 for your 6 percent discount bond, the current yield is 6.186 percent (6 divided by 97). If you pay 102 for a 6 percent bond, the current yield is 5.88 percent (6 divided by 102).

Current value   For most securities, Current Value = Quantity × Current Market Price.

Data mining   A technique for attempting to build predictive real-world models by discerning patterns in masses of historical data.

Debenture   An unsecured bond backed by the issuer's legally binding promise to pay.

Default   Failure to pay principal or interest in a timely manner.

Denomination   The face amount of a security.

Derivative   A financial instrument whose characteristics and value depend on the characteristics and value of an underlying investment, typically a bond, commodity, currency, or equity.

Discount   The percent by which the market value of a bond is less than par or face value.

Distressed stocks   Stocks with high book-to-market values and/or low price-to-earnings ratios. Another name for **Value stocks.**

Diversification   Dividing investment funds among a variety of investments with different risk/return characteristics to minimize portfolio risk.

DJIA   The Dow Jones Industrial Average, a U.S. large-cap stock index reflecting the performance of thirty very large stocks.

Duration   The percentage change in the price of a bond that can be expected given a percentage change in the yield on that bond. A higher duration number indicates a greater sensitivity of that bond's price to changes in interest rates.

EAFE Index   The Europe, Australasia, Far East Index consists of the stocks of companies from the developed EAFE countries. Very much like the S&P 500 Index, the stocks within the EAFE index are weighted by market capitalization.

Efficient frontier model   A model based on the assumption that investors care about the volatility of their portfolio, in addition to its expected return. The model computes portfolios (mixes of risky investments) that have the highest expected return for every attainable level of volatility.

Efficient market   A state in which trading systems fail to produce expected returns in excess of the market's overall rate of return, because everything currently knowable about a company is already incorporated into its stock price.

Efficient market hypothesis   A hypothesis that markets are efficient. (See Efficient market.)

Emerging markets   The capital markets of less-developed countries that are beginning to acquire characteristics of developed countries, such as higher per capita income. Countries typically included in this category would be Brazil, Mexico, Romania, Turkey, Thailand, and Korea.

Ending value   Value of the portfolio at the end of a specified period, such as the end of the quarter or the end of the year.

Event risk   The risk that something unexpected will occur (war, political crisis, flood, or hurricane) negatively impacting the value of a security.

Exchange traded funds (ETFs)   For practical purposes, these act like open-ended, no-load mutual funds. Like mutual funds, they can be created to represent virtually any index or asset class. They are not actually mutual funds. Instead, these new vehicles represent a cross between an exchange-listed stock and an open-ended, no-load mutual fund. Like stocks (but unlike mutual funds), they trade on a stock exchange throughout the day.

Ex-ante   Before the fact.

Expense ratio   The operating expenses of a mutual fund expressed as a percentage of total assets. These expenses are subtracted from the investment performance of a fund to determine the net return to shareholders. They cover manager fees, administrative costs, and, in some cases, marketing costs.

Ex-post   After the fact.

Foreign tax credit (FTC)   A tax credit used to reduce or eliminate double taxation when the same income is taxed in two countries.

Forward currency contract   An agreement to buy or sell a country's currency at a specific price, usually thirty, sixty, or ninety days in the future. This guarantees an exchange rate on a given date. It is typically used to hedge risk, such as currency risk.

Full faith and credit   The pledge that all taxing powers and resources, without limitation, will, if necessary, be used to repay a debt obligation.

Fundamental security analysis The attempt to uncover mispriced securities by focusing on predicting future earnings.

Futures contract An agreement to purchase or sell a specific collection of securities or a physical commodity at a specified price and time in the future. For example, an S&P 500 futures contract represents ownership interest in the S&P 500 Index, at a specified price for delivery on a specific date on a particular exchange.

Glamour stocks Stocks with low book-to-market values and/or high price-to-earnings ratios. Another name for **Growth stocks**.

Green investing Choosing to invest in companies having positive environmental records. Green investing is a special category of **Socially responsible** investing.

Growth stock Companies that have relatively high price-to-earnings (**P/E**) ratios or relatively low book-to-market (**BtM**) ratios (the opposite of value stocks) because the market anticipates rapid earnings growth, relative to the overall market. We are interested in a stock's earnings ratio because academic evidence indicates that investors can expect to be rewarded by investing in value companies' stocks. They are considered to be riskier investments (compared with growth companies' stocks), so investors demand a "risk premium" to invest in them.

Hedge fund A fund that generally has the ability to invest in a wide variety of asset classes. These funds often use leverage in an attempt to increase returns.

High-yield bond See **Junk bond.**

Hybrid security A security with both equity and fixed-income characteristics. Examples of hybrids are convertible bonds, preferred stocks, and junk bonds.

I bond A bond that provides both a fixed rate of return and an inflation protection component. The principal value of the bond increases by the total of the fixed rate and the inflation component. The income is deferred until funds are withdrawn from the account holding the bond.

Income Dividends and/or interest income.

Index fund A passively managed fund that seeks to replicate the performance of a particular index, such as the Wilshire 5000, the S&P 500, or the Russell 2000. The fund may replicate the index by buying and holding all the securities in that index in direct proportion to their weight (by market capitalization) within that index. The fund could sample the index (a common strategy for small-cap and total market index funds) and/or use index futures and other derivative instruments.

Internal rate of return (IRR) The Internal Rate of Return provides a measure of the growth of the portfolio in absolute terms. Size and timing of contributions and withdrawals of cash and securities influence IRR, as well as the performance of those securities. The IRR is useful for determining whether the portfolio is growing fast enough to meet future needs or goals. In the absence of capital flows, the **Time Weighted Rate of Return (TWR)** and the IRR are identical.

Investment gain Capital appreciation plus income, less fees and/or other expenses.

Initial public offering (IPO) The first offering of a company's stock to the public.

Investment grade A bond whose credit quality is at least adequate to maintain debt service. Moody's Investors Service investment grade ratings are Baa and higher. Standard & Poor's are BBB and higher. Below-investment-grade ratings suggest a primarily speculative credit quality.

Investment policy statement (IPS) This statement provides the investor's financial goals and the strategies employed to achieve them. Specific information on matters such as asset allocation, risk tolerance, and liquidity requirements should be included in the IPS. An IPS becomes more powerful if it is in writing, dated, and signed.

IRA A tax-advantaged individual retirement account.

Junk bond A bond rated below investment grade. Also referred to as a **High-yield bond.**

Kurtosis The degree to which exceptional values, much larger or smaller than the average, occur more frequently (high kurtosis) or less frequently (low kurtosis) than in a normal (bell shaped) distribution. High kurtosis results in exceptional values called "fat tails." Low kurtosis results in "thin tails."

Large-cap Large-cap stocks are those of companies considered big relative to other companies, as measured by their **Market capitalization.** Precisely what is considered a "large" company varies by source. For example, one investment professional may define it as having a market cap in excess of $2 billion, while another may use $5 billion.

Leverage The use of debt to increase the amount of assets that can be acquired (for example, to buy stock). Leverage increases the riskiness as well as the expected return of a portfolio.

Leveraged buy-out (LBO) An acquisition of a business using mostly debt and a small amount of equity. Assets of the business secure the debt.

Liquidity A measure of the ease of trading a security in the market.

Loser's game A game in which the odds of winning are so low it does not pay to play.

MAGI Modified adjusted gross income.

Management fees Total amount charged to an account for management of a portfolio.

Markdown The difference between a retail investor's selling price and the wholesale price (the price in the interdealer market).

Market cap/market capitalization For an individual stock, this is the total number of shares of common stock outstanding, multiplied by the current price per share. For example, if a company has 100 million shares outstanding and its current stock price is $30 per share, the market cap of this company is $3 billion.

Maturity The date on which the issuer promises to repay the principal.

Mean variance analysis The process of identifying optimal mean-variance portfolios, that is, portfolios with the highest expected return among all portfolios with the same variance/standard deviation; or equivalently, portfolios with the lowest variance/standard deviation among all portfolios with the same expected return.

Mezzanine financing A late-stage venture capital investment, usually the final round of financing prior to an IPO, typically used by companies expecting to go public within six to twelve months. The financing is usually structured to be repaid from proceeds of a public offering.

Micro-cap The smallest stocks by market capitalization: the ninth and tenth CRSP deciles. Other definitions used are the smallest 5 percent of stocks by market capitalization and stocks with a market capitalization of less than about $200 million.

Modern portfolio theory (MPT) A body of academic work founded on four concepts. First, markets are too efficient to allow expected returns in excess of the market's overall rate of return to be achieved consistently through trading systems. Active management is therefore counterproductive. Second, over sustained periods, asset classes can be expected to achieve returns commensurate with their level of risk. Riskier asset classes, such as small companies and value companies, will produce higher returns as compensation for their higher risk. Third, diversification across asset classes can increase returns and reduce risk. For any given level of risk, a portfolio can be constructed producing the highest expected return. Fourth, there is no one right portfolio for every investor. Each investor must choose an asset allocation that results in a portfolio with an acceptable level of risk for that investor's specific situation.

Monte Carlo simulation A method for approximating the answer to certain questions in mathematics, physics, and finance using statistical analysis (using a random number generator) where a direct answer in closed form is either not possible or exceptionally difficult to obtain.

Mortgage-backed security (MBS) A financial instrument representing an interest in a pool of mortgage loans.

MPT See **Modern portfolio theory.**

MSCI EAFE Index See **EAFE Index.**

NASDAQ The National Association of Securities Dealers Automated Quotations is a computerized marketplace in which securities are traded, frequently called the "over-the-counter market."

NAV For a mutual fund, its NAV is the total value of portfolio holdings minus the total value of all liabilities. The NAV is usually calculated on a daily basis and quoted per share. For example, "NAV is $14.68 per share."

Net contributions Cash deposits plus the market value of securities deposited into the portfolio, minus all cash withdrawals and the market value of securities transferred out.

Negative correlation When one asset experiences above average returns, the other tends to experience below average returns, and vice versa.

No-load A mutual fund that does not impose any charge for purchases or sales and has no 12(b)-1 fees.

Nominal returns Returns that have not been adjusted for inflation.

NYSE The New York Stock Exchange, which traces its origins to 1792, is the world's leading equities market. A broad spectrum of market participants, including listed companies, individual investors, institutional investors, and member firms participate in the NYSE market.

Other expenses In clients' reports from their advisers or broker/dealers, other expenses represent fees associated with transactions, such as SEC fees or postage and handling.

P/E ratio The ratio of stock price-to-earnings per share. Stocks with high P/E ratios are considered growth stocks; stocks with low P/E ratios are considered value stocks.

Par   One hundred percent of face value. Most bonds have a face value of $1,000. They are also traded in blocks of a minimum of $1,000. Par is considered $1,000.

Passive asset class funds   Mutual funds that buy and hold common stocks within a particular domestic or international asset class. The amount of each security purchased is typically in proportion to its capitalization relative to the total capitalization of all securities within the asset class. Each stock is held until it no longer fits the definition and guidelines established for remaining in that asset class. Passive asset class funds provide the building blocks needed to implement a passive management strategy.

Passive management   Passive management is a buy-and-hold investment strategy, specifically contrary to active management. Characteristics of the passive management approach include lower portfolio turnover, lower operating expenses and transactions costs, greater tax efficiency, consistent exposure to risk factors over time, and a long-term perspective.

Premium   The amount, if any, by which the price exceeds the principal amount (**par** value) of a bond.

Principal   The face value of a bond, exclusive of interest.

Prudent investor rule   A doctrine imbedded within the American legal code stating that a person responsible for the management of someone else's assets must manage those assets in a manner appropriate to the beneficiary's financial circumstances and tolerance for risk.

Purchases   In clients' reports from their advisers or broker/dealers, purchases represent the dollar amount of a particular position purchased during a specified period.

Put   An option contract giving the holder the right, but not obligation, to sell a security at a predetermined price on a specific date (European put) or during a specific period (American put).

Quantity   In clients' reports from their advisers or broker/dealers, the quantity represents the number of a security's shares, units, or option contracts held on the "as of" date.

Real returns   Returns adjusted for inflation.

Rebalancing   The process of restoring a portfolio towards its original asset allocation. Rebalancing can be accomplished either through adding newly investable funds or by selling portions of the best performing asset classes and using the proceeds to purchase additional amounts of the underperforming asset classes.

Real estate investment trust (REIT)   As represented by REITs, real estate is a separate asset class. REITs have their own risk and reward characteristics, as well as relatively low correlation with other equity and fixed-income asset classes. Investors can purchase shares of a REIT in the same way they would purchase other equities, or they can invest in a REIT mutual fund that is either actively or passively managed.

Redemption   The process of retiring existing bonds at or prior to maturity. It also refers to redeeming shares in a mutual fund by selling the shares back to the sponsor.

Registered investment adviser (RIA)   A designation that a financial consultant's firm is registered with the appropriate national (SEC) or state regulators and that the RIA representatives for that firm have passed required exams. RIA is not an accredited professional designation.

Reinvestment risk   The risk that future interest and principal payments, when received, will earn lower-than-current rates.

Risk premium   The higher expected (not guaranteed) return for accepting a specific type of nondiversifiable risk.

Russell 2000   The smallest 2,000 of the largest 3,000 publicly traded U.S. stocks. A common benchmark for small-cap stocks.

Retail funds   Mutual funds sold to the public, as opposed to institutional investors.

Sales/cash dividends   In clients' reports from their advisers or broker/ dealers, the dollar amount of a particular position sold during a specified period. This figure will include any dividends paid in cash.

Secondary market   The trading market for outstanding bonds and notes. This is an over-the-counter market and a free-form negotiated method of buying and selling, usually conducted by telephone or a trading system such as Bloomberg's.

Serial correlation   The correlation of a variable with itself over successive time intervals. Also known as autocorrelation.

Securities and Exchange Commission (SEC)   A government commission created by Congress to regulate the securities markets and protect investors. The SEC has jurisdiction over the operation of broker-dealers, investment advisers, mutual funds, and companies selling stocks and bonds to the investing public.

Sharpe ratio   A measure of the return earned above the rate of return on riskless one-month U.S. Treasury bills relative to the risk taken, with risk being measured by the standard deviation of returns. Example: The average return earned on an asset was 10 percent. The average rate of one-month Treasury bills was 4 percent. The standard deviation was 20 percent. The Sharpe Ratio would be equal to 10 percent minus 4 percent (6 percent), divided by 20 percent, or 0.3.

Short selling   Borrowing a security for the purpose of immediately selling it. This is done with the expectation that the investor will be able to buy the security back at a later date (and lower price), returning it to the lender and keeping any profit.

Skewness   A measure of the asymmetry of a distribution. Negative skewness occurs when the values to the left of (less than) the mean are fewer but *farther* from the mean than values to the right of the mean. For example: The return series of –30 percent, 5 percent, 10 percent, and 15 percent has a mean of 0 percent. There is only one return less than zero percent and three higher; but the negative one is much further from zero than the positive ones. Positive skewness occurs when the values to the right of (or more than) the mean are fewer but *farther* from the mean than are values to the left of the mean.

Small-cap   Small-cap stocks are those of companies considered small relative to other companies, as measured by their **Market capitalization.** Precisely what is considered a "small" company varies by source. For example, one investment professional may define it as having a market cap of less than $2 billion, while another may use $5 billion. We are interested in a stock's capitalization because academic evidence indicates that investors can expect to be rewarded by investing in smaller companies' stocks. They are considered to be riskier investments than larger companies' stocks, so investors demand a "risk premium" to invest in them.

Spread   The difference between the price a dealer is willing to pay for a bond (the bid) and the price at which a dealer is willing to sell a bond (the offer).

Socially responsible investing (SRI)   Investment strategy seeking to maximize both financial return and social good.

S&P 500 Index   A market-cap weighted index of 500 of the largest U.S. stocks, designed to cover a broad and representative sampling of industries.

Stable-value fund Fixed-income investment vehicles offered through defined contribution savings plans and IRAs. The assets in stable-value funds are *generally* high quality bonds and insurance contracts purchased directly from banks and insurance companies that guarantee to maintain the value of the principal and all accumulated interest. However, stable value funds may hold bonds of less than investment grade, as well as equities.

Standard deviation A measure of volatility or risk. The greater the standard deviation, the greater the volatility of a portfolio. Standard deviation can be measured for varying time periods, such as monthly, quarterly, or annually.

Style drift Style drift occurs when the portfolio moves away from its original asset allocation, either by the purchase of securities outside the particular asset class a fund represents or by not rebalancing to adjust for significant differences in performance of the various asset classes in the portfolio.

Subordinated debt A debt ranking below another liability in order of priority for payment of interest or principal.

Survivorship bias Funds that perform poorly close due to redemptions by investors or by being merged out of existence. Failing to include the performance data of all funds that existed during an analysis period—whether or not the funds disappeared—can skew results, making them appear better than the reality.

Sustainability investing An investment strategy recognizing companies that are moving society towards sustainability. It relies on a consensus-based scientific definition of sustainability developed by researchers at the Blekinge Institute of Technology in Sweden. It is a special category of Socially responsible investing.

Systematic risk Risk that cannot be diversified away. The market must reward investors for taking systematic risk, or they would not take it. That reward is in the form of a risk premium, a higher *expected* return than could be earned by investing in a less risky instrument.

Term to maturity The number of years left until the maturity date of a bond.

Three-factor model Differences in performance between diversified equity portfolios are best explained by the amount of exposure to the risk of the overall stock market, company size (market capitalization), and price (book-to-market [BtM] ratio) characteristics. Research has shown that, on average, the three factors explain more than 96 percent of the variation in performance of diversified U.S. stock portfolios.

Time weighted rate of return (TWR)   A rate-of-return measure of portfolio performance giving equal weight to each period regardless of any differences in amounts invested in each period. The TWR removes the impact caused by timing and the size of all capital flows. Because an investment manager typically has no control over contributions and withdrawals, the TWR is more suitable than the **Internal Rate of Return (IRR)** for determining the relative skill of the manager, or to compare to a market index or other managers. In the absence of capital flows, **TWR** and **IRR** are identical.

TIPS   See **Treasury Inflation-Protected Security.**

Tracking Error   The amount by which the performance of a fund differs from the appropriate index or benchmark. More generally, when referring to a whole portfolio, the amount by which the performance of the portfolio differs from a widely accepted benchmark, such as the S&P 500 Index or the Wilshire 5000 Index.

Transparency   The extent to which pricing information for a security is readily available to the general public.

Treasuries   Obligations carrying the full faith and credit of the U.S. government.

Treasury bills   Treasury instruments with a maturity of up to one year. Bills are issued at a discount to **par**. The interest is paid in the form of the price rising toward **par** until maturity.

Treasury bonds   Treasury instruments whose maturity is more than ten years.

Treasury notes   Treasury instruments whose maturity is more than one year, but not greater than ten.

Treasury inflation protected security (TIPS)   A bond that receives a fixed stated rate of interest, but also increases its principal by the changes in the Consumer Price Index. Its fixed interest payment is calculated on the inflated principal, which is eventually repaid at maturity.

Turnover   The trading activity of a fund as it sells securities and replaces them with new ones.

Uncompensated risk   Risk that can be diversified away, like the risk of owning a single stock or sector of the market. Since the risk can be diversified away, investors are not rewarded with a risk premium (higher expected return) for accepting this type of risk. Also called "unsystematic risk."

Unsecured bond A bond backed solely by a good faith promise of the issuer.

Unsystematic risk See **Uncompensated risk.**

Value stocks The stocks of companies with relatively low price-to-earnings **(P/E)** ratios or relatively high book-to-market **(BtM)** ratios: the opposite of growth stocks. The market anticipates slower earnings growth relative to the overall market. They are considered to be riskier investments than growth companies' stocks, so investors demand a "risk premium" to invest in them.

Variable annuity A life insurance annuity contract providing future payments to the holder. The size of the future payments will depend on the performance of the portfolio's securities, as well as the investor's age at the time of "annuitization" and prevailing interest rates.

Venture capital An investment in a start-up firm or small business prior to its initial public offering. Typically entails a high degree of risk.

Volatility The standard deviation of the change in value of a financial instrument within a specific time horizon. It is often used to quantify the risk of the instrument over that time period. Volatility is typically expressed in annualized terms.

Wash sale rule The tax code prohibits claiming a loss on the sale of an investment if a same, or a substantially similar, investment was purchased within thirty days before or after the sale date.

Weight Percentage value of a security or asset class held in a portfolio relative to the value of the total portfolio.

Yield curve Graph depicting the relationship between yields and current term to maturity for fixed-income investments with approximately the same default risk.

Zero-coupon bond A discount bond on which no current interest is paid. Instead, at maturity, the investor receives compounded interest at a specified rate. In taxable accounts, the difference between the discount price at purchase and the accreted value at maturity is not taxed as a capital gain, but is considered interest and usually taxed each year, not deferred until maturity.

Index

Management fees, 204
Mandell, Lewis, 181–182
Marginal utility of wealth, 20
Margins, to buy equities, 70
Markdown, 204
Market capitalization, 204, 208
Market exposure, 33
Market factors, 176
Markowitz, Harry, 5
Master limited partnerships (MLPs), 58
Maturity, 42–43, 204
   maturity risk of municipal bonds, 44
   reasons to increase risk, 43–44
   reasons to reduce risk, 43
Maverick Capital, 92
MBS. *See* Mortgage-backed security
MC. *See* Monte Carlo simulation
Mean variance analysis, 204
Medicaid, 189
Medicare, 150
Mezzanine financing, 204
Micro-cap, 204
MLPs. *See* Master limited partnerships
Models:
   capital asset pricing model, 175
   efficient frontier, 5–7
   Fama-French three-factor model, 22–23, 175–179, 209–210
Modern portfolio theory (MPT), 30, 91, 204–205
Modified adjusted gross income (MAGI), 204
   with Coverdell education savings accounts, 116
Monte Carlo (MC) simulation, 13, 14, 22, 38, 129–131, 141, 205
   results, 162
   withdrawals and, 158–160
Morgan Stanley, 92, 195–196
Morningstar, 196
Mortality credit, 126
Mortgage-backed security (MBS), 58–59, 205
Mortgages, 67–70
   borrowing limits, 186
   home-equity conversion, 187, 188
   prepayment versus increase tax-advantaged savings, 69–70
   reverse, 185–189
MPT. *See* Modern portfolio theory
MSCI EAGE Index, 29, 195–196. *See* EAFE index
Multiple asset class funds, 98
Municipal bonds, 44–46
   credit risk, 44
   maturity risk, 44

"Mutual-fund Performance: An Empirical Decomposition into Stock-Picking Talent, Style, Transaction Costs, and Expenses" (Wermers), 82
Mutual funds:
   actively managed, 93
   as benefit of passive investing, 91–92
   convenience and benefits of, 73
   diversification of, 74–75
   versus exchange-traded funds, 73
   fund selection criteria, 78–80
   larger versus smaller portfolio, 76
   leverage to increase returns, 78
   management of, 82
   performance of, 74
   versus securities, 73–80
   underperformance of, 4

NASDAQ. *See* National Association of Securities Dealers Automated Quotations
National Association of Securities Dealers Automated Quotations (NASDAQ), 205
National Center for Home Equity Conversion, 188
Natural rating, 41
NAV. *See* Net asset value
Negative correlation, 205
Net asset value (NAV), 73, 205
New York Stock Exchange (NYSE), 205
"Nobody Gains From Dollar Cost Averaging: Analytical, Numerical, and Empirical Results" (Knight and Mandell), 181–182
No-load, 205
Nominal returns, 205
"A Note on the SubOptimality of Dollar Cost Averaging as an Investment Policy" (Constantinides), 181–182
NYSE. *See* New York Stock Exchange

Odean, Terrance, 84
"On Persistence in Mutual-fund Performance" (Carhart), 82
Otten, Roger, 83

Parents and asset transfer, 168–169
Passive asset class funds, 206
Passive management, 206
P/E. *See* Price-to-earnings ratio
Pension Protection Act of 2006, 146–147
Pensions, 26
   management, 82–84

Treasury bonds, 76, 210
Treasury Inflation-Protected Security (TIPS), 210
  decision table for allocation and maturity of, 47
  reasons to decrease exposure to, 45–46
  reasons to increase exposure to, 45
  reasons to reduce maturity risk of, 43
  short-term income versus, 46–47
Treasury notes, 210
Tuition credits, 114–115
Turnover, 210
TWR. *See* Time Weighted Rate of Return

UGMA. *See* Uniform Gifts to Minors Act
Uncertainty:
  definition, 3
  versus risk, 4
Uncompensated risk, 210–211
Uniform Gifts to Minors Act (UGMA), 117
Uniform Prudent Investor Act, 91
Uniform Transfers to Minors Act (UTMA), 117
Universal and variable life insurance, 124
Unsecured bond, 211
Unsystematic risk. *See* Uncompensated risk
U.S. Department of Housing and Urban Development (HUD), 187
U.S. savings bonds, 117–118
U.S. Treasury, 59
U.S. versus international stocks, 28–30
UTMA. *See* Uniform Transfers to Minors Act

Value stocks, 31–34, 211
Value versus growth decision, 31–34

Vanguard Group, 92, 97
Vanguard High-Yield Fund, 56, 74, 78
Vanguard REIT mutual fund, 35
Variable annuities (VAs), 64–66, 211
VAs. *See* Variable annuities.
Venture capital (private equity), 61–62, 211
Verbrugge, James, 89–90
Volatility, 211
Vonnegut, Kurt, 20

Wahal, Sunil, 83–84
Wall Street Journal, 74
Wash sale rule, 104, 211
  avoiding, 108–109
Wealth, 26
Weight, 211
Wermers, Russ, 82
Whole life insurance, 123
Williams, Roy, 168, 169
Withdrawals, 157–165. *See also* Retirement
  in the absence of a Monte Carlo simulator, 160–163
  investment careers and, 37
  Monte Carlo simulations, 158–160
  required minimum distribution and, 140, 153
  safe withdrawal rate, 162–163
  sequencing, 163–165

Yale Endowment, 61
Yield curve, 211

Zero-coupon bond, 45, 211